D1222524

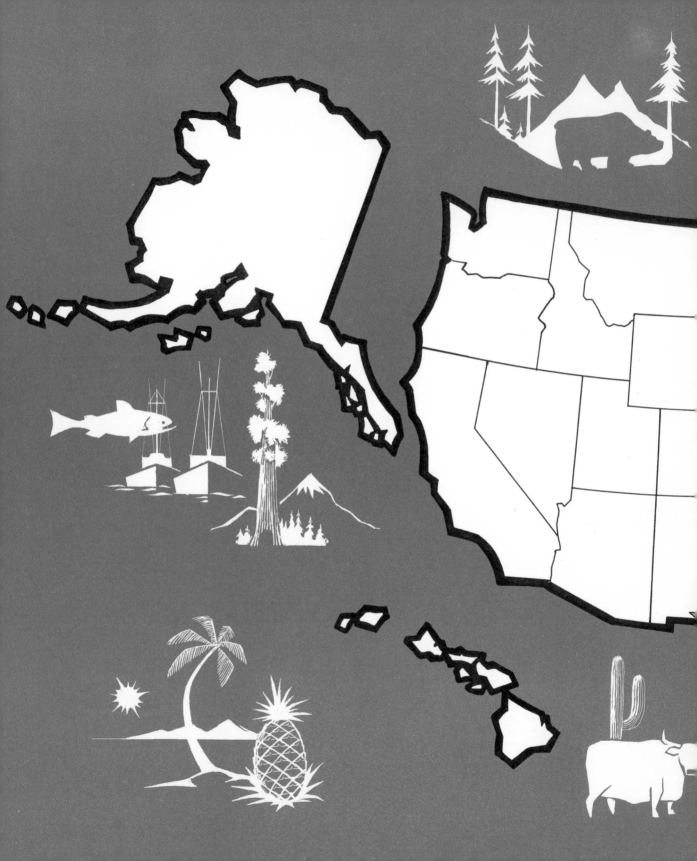

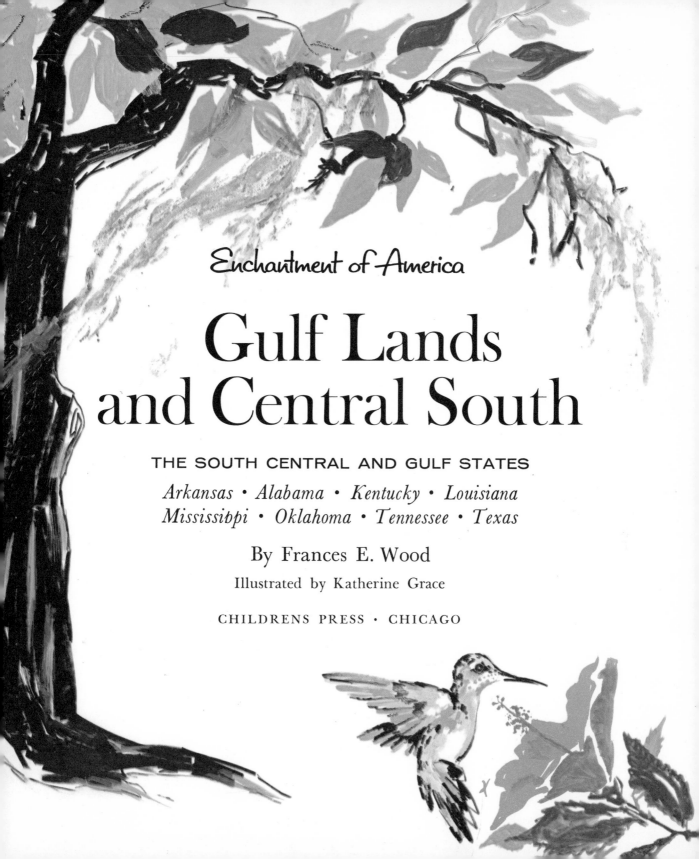

Enchantment of America

Gulf Lands and Central South

THE SOUTH CENTRAL AND GULF STATES

Arkansas • Alabama • Kentucky • Louisiana
Mississippi • Oklahoma • Tennessee • Texas

By Frances E. Wood

Illustrated by Katherine Grace

CHILDRENS PRESS • CHICAGO

Educational Consultant for the
Enchantment of America Series:
Marilyn M. Spore, Laboratory School,
University of Chicago

Regional Consultant for
GULF LANDS AND CENTRAL SOUTH:
Andrew Forest Muir, Ph.D.,
Lecturer in History,
Rice University

THIRD PRINTING
Library of Congress Catalog Card Number: 62-9076

Copyright, 1962, Childrens Press
Printed in the U.S.A.

Contents

Location

Lying between the Middlewestern and Plains States on the north and the Gulf of Mexico on the south is a great expanse of land made up of mountains and plains. Here are the South Central and Gulf States—Kentucky, Tennessee, Alabama, Missisippi, Louisiana, Arkansas, Oklahoma, and Texas. These states combine the grace and beauty and warmth of the deep South with the wide-open spaces and colorful life of the West.

Formation and Change

For millions of years this land was covered by shallow seas. At times the land rose and the seas withdrew, only to rush in again when the land sank. Each time the sea returned, it spread another layer of mud and sand, or sediment, on the land.

At first there was very little life in the sea. Then tiny sea plants and animals, many of which had shells, appeared. The skeletons of these plants and animals became part of the mud and slime at the bottom of the sea. As more and more layers of sediment were laid down, the layers underneath were compressed into rock, some of which we know today as limestone and sandstone.

9

As time went on, the plants and animals of the sea became larger and larger. Some animals crawled about on the bottom or burrowed through the mud. Fish swam in the water. After millions of years, amphibians developed. These were four-legged animals that could live both in water and on the land. Some of the amphibians were small and some were as large as alligators. Some of them could climb the trees which flourished wherever the land was not covered by water. Frogs and giant salamanders and other amphibians lived in and out of the water. Huge insects crawled on the ground and flew about in the air.

Tree-like ferns and many other plants, large and small, grew in the swamps and bogs. As the land sank again, the sea came in and covered the plants under heavy layers of mud and sand and water. During long periods of time, this happened again and again. The land rose and the seas retreated. Forests flourished. Then the land sank, the seas returned, and the forests were again covered. Little by little, the plants were compressed by the weight of the water and sediment on top of them into a black rock that we call coal. When miners dig coal out of the ground today, they often find the outlines, or fossils, of ferns and other plants in the coal.

Sometime during this coal-forming age, reptiles appeared. These animals, like the amphibians, laid eggs and could live in water as well as on land. A thick layer of red sandstone in north-central Texas,

called the Redbeds, contains the fossils of amphibians and reptiles. The Redbeds show that these amphibians and reptiles lived at the same time and probably preyed on each other. Some of the reptiles were ten to fifteen feet long and had huge, sail-like fins on their backs.

During all this time, as the sea came in and covered large portions of the land, retreated, and came in again, new layers of sediment were laid down. More and more pressure was put on the limestone and sandstone and other rocks underneath. At last the pressure became so great that the earth's crust gave way, and some of the layers of rock were pushed up into high, rugged mountains not far from the Atlantic Coast.

In the course of time, these mountains were worn away, or eroded, by the forces of wind and rain and running water. Sediment from the mountains was spread over the land. Finally, a little farther west, the present Appalachian Mountains were pushed up in much the same way that the earlier mountains had been formed. When the Appalachians were first formed, they were much higher and more rugged than they are now. They, too, have been worn down by the forces of nature.

Still farther west, and still later, the "Folded Appalachians" were pushed up—great ridges with valleys between, that ran for hundreds of miles toward the northeast and southwest. Rivers traveled many of the valleys and sometimes cut across the ridges in "water gaps." All along the western side of this ridge and valley country, there was less folding, and the land was raised into a high, more-or-less level plateau. Rivers began to run toward the east and toward the west, washing valleys as they went. So now, instead of a regular northeast-southwest direction, the ridges and valleys of the plateau go in all directions, and the rivers flowing in the valleys drain in all directions, too. The Cumberland Plateau is part of this great plateau country. Through the plateau flow the Tennessee and Cumberland rivers, winding back and forth between the ridges to find their way to the Ohio River.

After the mountains were formed, seas came up from the south Atlantic Ocean and the Gulf of Mexico across the extreme south end of the Appalachians and west of them as far north as southern Illinois. The seas spread sediment over all the area, building up the Atlantic and Gulf Coastal plains.

Early Inhabitants of the Land

By this time many strange reptiles had developed, some of which lived on land and some in the water. Some had wings and could fly. Dinosaurs appeared, small ones at first, and then huge creatures that ruled the land and water. Many of the large dinosaurs were peaceful, harmless creatures that lived on plants. Others ate flesh and preyed on their neighbors. Some walked erect on their hind legs, while others went about on all fours.

13

During the dinosaur reign, a few small mammals appeared. These were warm-blooded, four-legged animals and were usually covered with hair. Their young were born alive instead of being hatched from eggs. Birds had also developed by this time.

About sixty million years ago, as the sea withdrew for the last time and the climate became somewhat cooler, mammals spread all over the land and the dinosaurs disappeared. Only a few reptiles remained, such as crocodiles and turtles.

There was a great variety of mammals. The first ones were small, rather stupid creatures, but, like the reptiles, they became larger and larger. The horse started as a tiny animal, only a foot high, with four toes on the front feet, three on the hind ones. Slowly, through the ages, the toes developed into one hoof on each foot, and some horses became even larger than the ones we know today.

Among the large mammals that lived in North America were huge beasts with as many as six bony knobs, resembling horns, on their heads. Others had only two horn-like structures on their noses and looked like giant rhinoceroses. As millions of years went by, the older animals died out and new ones appeared—camels, rhinoceroses, deer, giant sloths, saber-toothed cats, mastodons, and mammoths. There were sea mammals, too. The remains of whale-like animals as much as seventy feet long have been found near the Atlantic Coast and in Alabama.

About one million years ago, the climate in North America began to change. It became much cooler in the north, and so much snow fell that all of it could not melt. Instead, it packed into a great ice sheet, which, of its own weight, began moving slowly southward. It reached as far south as the Ohio River and southern Illinois and forced most of the animals into the southern states. Only a few kinds were hardy enough to feed along the edges of the ice.

The ice sheet came down into the interior of the continent at least four times. Each time it melted back into the north and then returned, covering the plants and driving the animals ahead of it into warmer climates. The last time the ice sheet came was about 25,000 years ago, and the last of it melted from the extreme northern United States and southern Canada probably 10,000 years ago. By the end of the Ice Age, or shortly thereafter, most of the giant mammals had died out.

The Lay of the Land Today

The vast stretch of land that is the South Central and Gulf region reaches down from the 6,000-foot peaks of the Appalachians to the low interior and Gulf Coastal plains and the Mississippi Valley. Then it rises to the mountains of Arkansas and the High Plains of western Oklahoma and Texas.

The mountains, valleys and ridges, and the plateaus of the Appalachians swing down through the eastern part of the South Carolina region and come to an end in northern Alabama. Along the eastern edge of Tennessee and extending into North Carolina are the Great Smoky Mountains—those beautiful tree-covered mountains over which an eternal blue mist hovers. The Great Smokies merge on the east with the Blue Ridge. West of these high mountain ranges, folded ridges and valleys run northwest and southeast. The widest of the valleys is called the Great Valley; its southern end is the Tennessee Valley.

The Cumberland Plateau, west of the ridge and valley section, extends through Kentucky and Tennessee into Alabama. This plateau has been deeply cut by rivers, and contains rugged mountain gorges. The eastern edge is bordered by the Cumberland and Pine Mountain ranges, with Cumberland Gap at the corner where Virginia meets Kentucky and Tennessee. The Wilderness Road, traveled by early pioneers, went through this notch in the mountains. Highways and railroads go through it today.

The Gulf Coastal Plain forms the southern portion of the South Central and Gulf States and meets the interior lowlands that come down from the north, west of the Appalachians. Winding its way southward through the interior lowlands and the central Gulf Coastal Plain is the wide valley of the Mississippi, North America's mightiest river. In the southern states the river meanders through a wide flood plain, often changes its course, and sometimes cuts across its loops to form oxbow lakes. In many places along its course, levees have been built in an attempt to prevent floods during periods of high water. At the mouth of the Mississippi, where it empties into the Gulf of Mexico, is a wide delta, built up by the silt brought down by the river through countless ages.

West of the Mississippi the southern extension of the Ozark Highland, called the Boston Mountains, occupies northwestern Arkansas and extends into Oklahoma. South of the Boston Mountains, in both states, are the highly scenic Ouchita Mountains. Also in Oklahoma are the Arbuckle and Wichita Mountains, the low, eroded stumps of what were once lofty mountains.

The High Plains, reaching several thousand feet in altitude, extend from western Oklahoma, through the Texas Panhandle, to the Gulf Coastal Plain. The northern part of this area, in Texas, is often called the *Llano Estacado,* or Staked Plain. The southeastern part is the Edwards Plateau. West of the Pecos River is an area of high mountains, deep canyons, and arid valleys and deserts.

Most of the rivers of the South Central and Gulf States drain into the Gulf of Mexico by way of the Mississippi River and the Rio Grande. Many of these rivers were flood menaces in times of high water, but they have been largely tamed by numerous dams. These dams, besides backing up the water into large lakes, provide sites for hydroelectric plants that furnish power for the South's greatly increased manufacturing industries.

Along the Gulf Coast are barrier islands with wide, sandy beaches.

Climate

The climate of the Gulf Lands and Central South varies widely. It ranges all the way from humid, subtropical conditions in the deep South to winter blizzards in the semiarid High Plains.

The deep South has long, hot summers and short, mild winters, with a long growing season and plenty of rain. Along the Gulf Coast, sea breezes moderate the temperatures and give the area a pleasant climate both in summer and winter. Palm trees and citrus fruits and beautiful tropical flowers flourish in the lower Rio Grande Valley in Texas. However, devastating hurricanes sometimes sweep the coast, such as the hurricane of September, 1961, which caused property damage in the millions of dollars.

To the north, in Tennessee and Kentucky, the climate is mild, with little snow except in the mountains. The western High Plains are semiarid, with high winds. Severe droughts, especially in the western part of Oklahoma's Panhandle, can cause "Dust Bowl" conditions such as those of the 1930's. Desert conditions prevail in the corner of Texas that is west of the Pecos River.

18

Things to think about

How were the mountains in the South Central and Gulf States made?

How was the great coal and petroleum wealth of this region formed?

How did amphibians, reptiles and mammals develop in this region?

Describe the topography of the present-day Gulf Lands and Central South. What are the major land forms of this region?

Why does this region have a variety of climates? What are these different climates?

19

People come to the central south

The First People

Sometime during the last Ice Age, man entered the New World. He came into Alaska from Siberia by way of Bering Strait, a distance of about fifty miles. At times, so much water was locked up on the land in the form of ice that the level of the sea was considerably lower than it is now. Scientists believe that during such times there was a land bridge across the Bering Strait. At other times ice thick enough to walk on stretched between the two points of land.

The first people to cross over were probably a band of hunters following herds of giant bison or mammoths. In Alaska they found rich hunting, for many different kinds of animals were feeding on the lush grass of the Yukon Valley, which was free from ice. More and more people crossed into the New World. Some of them followed wandering herds down river valleys and through mountain passes.

Along the east side of the Rockies was a corridor, two hundred miles wide in places, that was free from ice. Many of the people moved south through this corridor and reached other land where there was no ice. Then they spread throughout what is now the southern part of the United States. Some continued south into Mexico and Central and South America, where they gradually built up, through thousands of years, the great Aztec, Mayan, and Incan civilizations.

The story of these people and their migrations is told in the charred remains of campfires buried twenty feet and more under the ground. These and other remains have been dug up all the way from Alaska to the tip of South America. Spearheads have been found with the bones of animals that disappeared during the Ice Age.

A woman's skull, believed to be at least 12,000 years old, was dug up near Midland, Texas, and the skeleton of a young girl was found in Minnesota in a layer of earth that was laid down 20,000 years ago. Spearheads with carefully chipped, fluted edges were excavated in Texas and other places in the United States east of the Rockies. They are called Folsom points because they were first found with the bones of Ice Age animals near Folsom, New Mexico. Older spearheads, called Clovis points, have also been found.

Caves have been found which were used by prehistoric Indians through the centuries. Russell Cave, in northern Alabama near the Tennessee line, contains layer after layer of relics of all sorts. Near the surface was found pottery that was made by the Woodland Indians during the colonial period of North America. As the scientists dug deeper, they found relics that ranged from a few hundreds of years to thousands of years in age. Bone needles, arrowheads, spear points, even skeletons of the people, were among the things that were excavated. At 23 feet were the charred remains of a campfire that was probably 9,000 years old; at 35 feet, the remains of another fire that was possibly 12,000 years old.

Relics that are typical of Indians of the north and of the south indicate that this cave may have been a stopping place for Indians traveling in each direction. Russell Cave is now a national monument.

The giant bison, mastodons, mammoths, and many of the other large animals became extinct during the Ice Age or shortly after it. Horses, which had migrated from North America to Siberia, disappeared from the New World and were not seen here again until the Spaniards brought some to this continent thousands of years later. Big game hunting was at an end, and the people had to rely for food on wild plant life and small game.

Sometime, no one knows just when or how, some of the Indians learned to cultivate wild plants, such as corn, beans, squash, and tobacco. A new way of life began. Instead of wandering from place to place in search of game, people settled down in small villages and cultivated garden patches, harvesting their produce in the fall and storing it in safe places for the winter. They also gathered wild berries and nuts and the roots of wild plants. The men fished in nearby streams, hunted deer, and snared rabbits and other small game.

The Mound Builders

Possibly a thousand years before the time of Christ, a strange culture developed in the Mississippi Valley and spread over the eastern half of what is now the United States. We call the people who practiced this culture *Mound Builders* because of the mounds they constructed, but we do not know who the Indians were who started the culture nor where they came from. There were really many different kinds of people who built different kinds of mounds over a period of hundreds of years. The excavation of some of the mounds and examination of the many articles found in them have told us much about these prehistoric peoples, but there is nothing to tell us where they came from or where they went.

The first mounds were built in the upper Mississippi Valley and spread from there eastward and as far south as Kentucky and Tennessee—thousands and thousands of them. The mounds were in many different sizes and shapes. Some were in squares and circles and other geometric forms; others were shaped like animals and birds. When these mounds were excavated, skeletons of people were found in many of them, and so they are called "burial mounds."

Some of these people were important chiefs. The many valuable articles that were buried with them—copper headdresses and breast plates, burial robes embroidered with pearls, tobacco pipes carved from stone, jewelry, and many others—show that the Mound Builders had great artistic ability and a high degree of civilization.

As a rule, the mound builders lived in villages near their mounds. Their houses were usually round and covered with grass or mats. Often a high fence or stockade surrounded the village. The sites of many of these villages have been excavated and broken pottery and other household articles have been found.

Many hundreds of years after the first burial mounds were erected, a new kind of mound, the temple mound, appeared. The building of mounds of this type started in the lower Mississippi Valley and spread throughout the area that is now the southeastern states. A few of these mounds have been found as far north as Illinois and southern Wisconsin. A large group of them is at Moundville, Alabama.

The temple mounds are quite different from the burial mounds. They are flat-topped rectangular mounds, and many are so large that it must have taken thousands of workers many years to build each of them. Since there was no machinery in these early times, not even wheelbarrows, and no beasts of burden, all of the dirt for these great mounds had to be carried in baskets, some of it for long distances. There must have been a very good reason for these people to work so hard.

Apparently these new Mound Builders were sun worshippers and their temples to the sun were built on the tops of the mounds. Since they were made of wood, the temples rotted away through the centuries and only the earthen bases were left. The first Spanish explorers in the sixteenth century saw some of the temple mounds in the making, but

the temples were gone and the Mound Builders had disappeared by the time later explorers and the first settlers entered the area.

The temple mounds were somewhat similar in appearance and use to the great stone pyramids and mounds of the Aztec and Mayan Indians of Mexico and Central and South America. In burial grounds surrounding the temples, many treasures were buried in the graves of important leaders. The carving and art work on these treasures also resemble that of Mexico. So it is believed that the culture of the temple-mound builders may have come into the Mississippi Valley from Mexico.

Nobody knows what became of any of the mound-building people. Perhaps they were absorbed by more primitive tribes that moved into the region. The Natchez Indians of Mississippi may have been direct descendants of the temple-mound builders. This Indian nation lived near the huge Emerald Mound and worshipped the sun. They had two classes, the aristocracy and the common people, and their ruler, called "the Sun," was considered so sacred that he was carried around on a litter and not allowed to touch foot to the ground. The Natchez nation was destroyed in wars with the French.

The Spanish Search for Gold

Inspired by Christopher Columbus' voyages of discovery between 1492 and 1502, Spanish explorers sought the mainland of North America and visited the Texas coast as early as 1519. Some years later, Spanish colonists sailing for Florida were wrecked on the Texas coast. One of their leaders, Cabeza de Vaca, and three companions were captured by the Indians and lived among them for a number of years. They finally escaped and made their way through Texas to Mexico, where Hernán Cortés had conquered the Aztecs.

De Vaca's stories of the Indian villages he had visited and the buffalo he had seen, which he called "hunchbacked cattle," caused Cortés to send explorers into this new country. One of these was Francisco Coronado, who crossed Texas and the panhandle of Oklahoma into Kansas in 1541. Coronado was looking for fabulous golden cities where he expected to find much gold and precious stones. He found no gold or gems, however—only primitive Indian villages—and he returned to Mexico in disgust.

About this time another Spanish expedition, also in search of gold, was coming from the East Coast. This one was led by Hernando de Soto, who was sure that he could find much wealth in the new land. He started out from Florida with a force of about six hundred men, two hundred horses, and a large number of pigs, which he was taking along to provide meat for the expedition. For two years he explored the southern states, fighting his way through swamps and thick forests. After exploring what is now Mississippi and Tennessee, he reached the bank of a mighty river—the first white man to set eyes on the Mississippi.

De Soto's army crossed the river in boats that they built from trees along the bank. For another year the Spaniards explored the land west of the Mississippi, but they found no gold—nothing but unfriendly Indians, to whom the Spaniards were very cruel. Many of the men died from malaria or were killed by the Indians. Many horses were lost. At last, discouraged and ill, De Soto returned to the Mississippi River. Here he died and was buried in the dark waters of the river late at night, because his men did not want the Indians to know that the expedition had lost its leader. Then the Spaniards built more boats and floated in them down the river to the Gulf, and finally made their way to Mexico.

27

The French Explore and Settle

The next man to explore the lower Mississippi came from the north a hundred and forty years later. He was the Frenchman Robert Cavalier, Sieur de la Salle, who, having heard of the mighty river that emptied into the sea, determined to explore it to its very end. With a force of fifty men, he crossed the Great Lakes, traveled down the Illinois River to the Mississippi, and then floated down it to its mouth at the Gulf of Mexico. Here he erected a cross and proclaimed that all the land drained by the Mississippi and its tributaries was the possession of King Louis XIV. So France claimed all the land on both sides of the Mississippi River, and Spain claimed the area that is now Texas.

Colonists came from France to settle the new land, but malaria took the lives of many of the newcomers, and other wilderness hardships made settlement slow. Mobile was founded in 1710; Fort St. Jean Baptiste was established in 1714 and later became Natchitoches, Louisiana's first permanent settlement. New Orleans was founded four years later and very soon became an important shipping point.

England Gains Possession of the Land

Meanwhile a series of four wars was going on between England and France, and these spread to the New World. When the last one ended, in 1763, the French ceded all their land in the New World east of the Mississippi River to England. They had already ceded their possessions west of the river, called Louisiana, to Spain.

Daniel Boone

Even before the end of these wars fur traders, explorers and hunters from the English colonies crossed the mountains into the Kentucky and Tennessee country. Daniel Boone, noted hunter and scout, was one of these. With his brother, he spent over a year hunting and exploring the new country. Boone returned to his home in North Carolina with glowing accounts of the wonderful land beyond the mountains where the grass grew lush and tall, and the wild game was the finest to be found anywhere.

In 1775 Boone, with thirty companions, hacked out the trail through the Cumberland Gap known as the Wilderness Road, and led a band of settlers over it to found Boonesboro in Kentucky. A survey party led by James Harrod had already surveyed for the town of Harrodstown, now Harrodsburg, oldest town in the state.

At the end of the Revolutionary War, all the land east of the Mississippi became the property of the new American nation. Pioneers continued to pour into it, in spite of bloody wars with the Indians who resented the settlers moving into their hunting grounds. Little by little the Indians were subdued, but it was many years before the Indian problems were finally settled.

The Louisiana Purchase

As new farms and settlements developed in the rich land west of the Appalachians, the farmers had another problem. That was how to get their products to market. There were as yet no roads across the mountains. The only way to get products to market was to float them in flatboats down the Mississippi River to New Orleans, where they could be loaded on ships and sent to the cities on the East Coast.

But New Orleans and the Mississippi were controlled by the Spanish, who were not very friendly to American shippers. Conditions were no better when the French emperor, Napoleon, forced Spain to return Louisiana to France. In 1803, Thomas Jefferson, President of the United States, solved the problem by buying all of Louisiana from Napoleon for $15,000,000. This is known as the "Louisiana Purchase." Now all the land in the South Central and Gulf region, except Texas, belonged to the United States.

Five Civilized Tribes

Prominent among the Indians who inhabited the southern part of the United States at the time of the Louisiana Purchase were the Creeks, Cherokees, Chickasaws, Choctaws, and Seminoles. These were agricultural Indians, rather than nomads. They lived in villages and farmed the land around them. Early in the nineteenth century these Indians adopted the white man's ways, farmed as he did, built good houses, and acquired cattle and other livestock. Some of them owned Negro slaves and had cotton and tobacco plantations. Many of the women had spinning wheels and wove cotton into cloth.

Few of these Indians could read or write, however, because they found English hard to learn and they did not have a written language of their own. Then a wonderful thing happened. A half-breed Cherokee whose Indian name was Sequoyah invented a Cherokee alphabet. This he did by making up some symbols and combining them with English letters.

The Indians found this alphabet easy to use, and were soon reading and writing in Cherokee. They wrote letters to each other and published a newspaper in both Cherokee and English, named the *Cherokee Phoenix.* The Bible was printed in both languages, too. Then they printed their laws and adopted a constitution based on the white man's constitution. People began calling these Indians the "Five Civilized Tribes."

But more and more white settlers were moving into the area and taking more and more of the Indians' land. After a few of the Indians had agreed to move to new land west of the Mississippi River, the United States government determined to move all of them into an area then called Indian Territory—now the state of Oklahoma. Many of the Indians refused to move, and there was a long struggle between them and the government before they finally started for Oklahoma. The march was badly mismanaged, and many of the Indians died on "The Trail of Tears," as it was called.

Osage Indians and others were already living in Oklahoma, and the government also moved some Plains tribes there.

The land allotted to the Five Civilized Tribes was good and they again began a civilized way of life. Each tribe maintained its own government, with its own constitution and laws. They established homes, founded schools, and published the first newspaper in Oklahoma. Eventually, however, the white man moved into Oklahoma and again took over and the Indian nations were broken up.

Texas Joins the Union

In the meantime, things were happening in Texas, too. In 1821, the same year that Mexico won her freedom from Spain, Texas was opened to colonization by Americans and thousands of families moved into the Mexican state. Among the famous Americans who went to Texas were Stephen A. Austin, Davy Crockett, Jim Bowie, William Travis, and Sam Houston.

The Americans' ideas of freedom and self-government were different from those of the Mexicans, however, and it was not long until trouble arose. In the war that resulted, the Mexican army stormed the Alamo, an old mission which the Texans were using as a fort, and killed all of the men in it. Among the slain Americans were Davy Crockett, Jim Bowie, and William Travis.

The Mexicans, led by Santa Anna, the dictator of Mexico, wiped out other Texas forces. Then the tide turned. The Texas army, led by Sam Houston and spurred on by the war cry, "Remember the Alamo!" completely crushed the Mexican army in the Battle of San Jacinto and took Santa Anna prisoner.

A flag with one star was raised over the Republic of Texas, and Sam Houston was elected the first president of this nation. At this election, the people also voted to ask the United States to annex Texas, but it was almost ten years later, December 29, 1845, when the Lone Star State was admitted to the Union as the twenty-eighth state.

Things to think about

What caused the first people to cease their wanderings and settle in small villages?

What were the differences between the burial mounds and the temple mounds?

Why did the Spanish and the French first come to the Gulf Lands and Central South?

How did white settlement come to the vast lands west of the Appalachians?

How were the "Five Civilized Tribes" different from other Indians?

How did Texas become one of the United States?

The Central south and gulf lands today

Natural Resources

A wide variety of soil and plenty of water, except in the extreme western section, are two of the most important resources of the South Central and Gulf States. Two of the greatest rivers on the continent, the Mississippi and the Rio Grande, flow through this region. Huge, man-made lakes on many of the tributaries store the water for use where it is most needed and furnish power for industry.

The South has large reserves of natural gas and petroleum, and iron, coal, limestone, sulfur, and salt are also found in large amounts. Forests grow in most of the states, and the fine scenery and great variety of plant and animal life attract a growing tourist trade.

Farm and Ranch Lands

The great range of climate and variety of soils make possible the production of almost every kind of crop grown in the United States. Cotton, however, is still king, with corn a close second.

Before the Civil War the agriculture of the deep South was largely a one-crop industry. Cotton was grown everywhere, with large plantations worked by Negro slaves predominating. Land was cheap and fertilizers unknown. When the soil was depleted, the cotton grower moved on to other land. The abandoned land became deeply eroded, and unfit for growing any kind of crop.

During the Civil War many of the plantation homes were burned and the land ravaged. After the war, many of the owners were so impoverished that they had to sell out for whatever they could get. Cotton continued to be the principal crop, but now much of the land was exhausted and eroded. The invasion of the boll weevil added to the planters' distress.

But a new day has dawned in the South. Scientific methods of growing cotton have been adopted, and fertilizers are used. Much of the eroded land has been terraced or planted with trees or grass. Diversified crops are grown, such as corn, oats, hay, soybeans, vegetables, and fruits.

35

Tobacco is a leading crop, especially in Tennessee and Kentucky, and some of the southern states are noted for their production of pecans, peanuts, and sweet potatoes or "yams." Tung trees are another interesting southern agricultural product. A drying oil made from the nuts of this tree is used in making printing ink, varnishes, and other similar products.

Oklahoma is a leading state in the production of broomcorn. Louisiana produces sugar cane. Rice is an important crop in the irrigated coastal areas of Texas and Louisiana and in the irrigated interior lowlands of Arkansas. The lower Rio Grande Valley, in Texas, is becoming famous for its citrus fruits and other fruits and vegetables, and winter wheat is important in western Texas and Oklahoma.

Texas started the beef industry in the United States early in the nineteenth century with the wild cattle known as Texas longhorns. These had developed from cattle that had escaped from the Spaniards in the early days of exploration and roamed the plains in vast numbers. Then Herefords, Shorthorns, and other breeds were introduced. Today, these are being crossed with Brahmas, which makes them immune to tick fever and also makes better beef.

Between eight and nine million head of cattle are raised in Texas every year. Many of the huge cattle holdings of the early days have been broken up into smaller ranches now, but some large ranches still remain. The famous King Ranch still has nearly one million acres, in three separate pieces.

Since so much formerly eroded land has been planted with grass and hay, a thriving cattle industry has spread to other southern states as well. Sheep, hogs, horses, and mules are also raised in large numbers.

Forests and Fisheries

In pioneering days, many of the forests were ruthlessly destroyed to make way for the cultivation of cotton, but a program of scientific reforestation and lumbering has restored this resource to the South. Now magnificent hardwood and pine forests cover much of the southern states. These forests furnish great quantities of the nation's hardwood lumber, as well as pine lumber, pulpwood, and such by-products as turpentine, tar, and resin. Spanish moss, which hangs from many of the trees in the subtropical areas, is used for making upholstery and mattresses.

Salt-water fishing is an important industry in the Gulf States, and Louisiana and Mississippi's shrimp and oyster fleets are famous. Each year in August, a colorful ceremony is held in Biloxi Bay just before the start of shrimp fishing, when the fishing boats gather in a quiet cove for the blessing of the fleet. Much of the shrimp and oyster take is packed or canned in the coastal cities and shipped to other sections of the United States.

Salt-water fish are caught in large quantities along the coast, and include speckled trout, red snappers, mackerel, and menhaden, a fish that is used to make oil and fertilizers. Salt-water sport fishing off the coast and fresh-water fishing in the large man-made lakes have become a great tourist attraction.

Mining

The South Central States have several important and interesting mineral resources, but the widespread discovery of oil and natural gas has dwarfed all others. The oil fields of Texas yield forty per cent of all the oil produced in the United States, and the state also leads in the production of natural gas. Louisiana and Oklahoma have vast oil and gas fields, and lesser quantities are present in almost all of the other states. Oil wells are found even on Oklahoma's capitol grounds in Oklahoma City. Oil discoveries on their lands have brought wealth to many of the state's Indians. Tulsa and Houston are famous oil centers and oil refineries form an important part of the industry of many other cities. Much of the oil and gas is carried through large underground pipes to the Great Lakes area and the northeast.

Coal is found in Alabama and the four northernmost states of the South Central region. Iron ore and limestone are also found near the coal beds of Alabama. The nearness of these three necessary minerals enables Birmingham and nearby cities to make low-cost steel. Zinc is an important mineral in Oklahoma, Arkansas, and Tennessee. Texas and Louisiana produce most of the sulfur in the United States. Arkansas, which furnishes ninety per cent of the country's bauxite, used for making aluminum, also has the only diamond mine in the United States. Ninety per cent of the country's supply of helium, a gas used for inflating balloons and other things, is produced in the Texas panhandle.

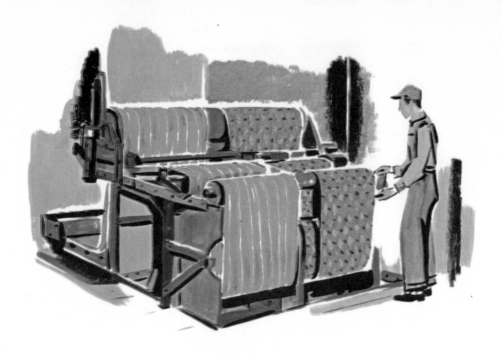

Manufacturing and Processing

The change from an agricultural South to an industrial South has been an astonishing one. For many years the whole southern economy depended on the growing of cotton, which was baled and shipped to factories in the northeastern United States or to England to be made into cloth. There were few factories in the South because there was no way to generate low-cost power to run machinery.

Then the Tennessee Valley Authority, known as the "TVA," entered the picture and built numerous high dams on the rivers of the Tennessee Basin. These dams supply enough cheap power to run factories and processing plants throughout the South Central States. The discovery of natural gas in many areas also helps to supply low-cost fuel. Now much of the cotton is made into cloth near where it is grown. Furniture factories and paper mills operate near the source of supply. Meat-packing plants, cheese factories, vegetable and fruit canneries have sprung up. Leather goods, chemicals, and fertilizers are manufactured, and shipbuilding is becoming an important industry.

Manufacturers and printing companies are moving down from the North to be near the source of raw materials. Many areas are setting aside industrial parks, with sites for large and small industrial plants.

The South has a vital share in the manufacture of materials necessary for national defense and in the atomic-energy program. Oak Ridge, near Knoxville, Tennessee, is a city of nearly 30,000 people which was founded by the national government during the Second World War and kept secret until the end of the war. It is the site of the Oak Ridge National Laboratory, which developed materials for the atomic bomb during the war, and now produces radio-active materials for industrial and medical uses. An atomic-energy museum contains over thirty exhibits, and is the only one of its kind in the world. A group of southern universities has formed the Oak Ridge Institute of Nuclear Studies to work with the laboratory.

Transportation

The South Central and Gulf States have plenty of railroads, airlines, and fine highways, but the story of transportation is linked closely to their waterways. First the Indians and then the explorers and settlers used the waterways to penetrate the region. The first French explorers went down the Mississippi from the Great Lakes. Later the French went up the rivers from Mobile Bay and New Orleans to establish forts and trading posts and settlements.

Many of the settlers floated down the Ohio and Mississippi rivers in flatboats and keelboats, and entered the interior by way of the rivers. Farmers sent their produce to market on the waterways.

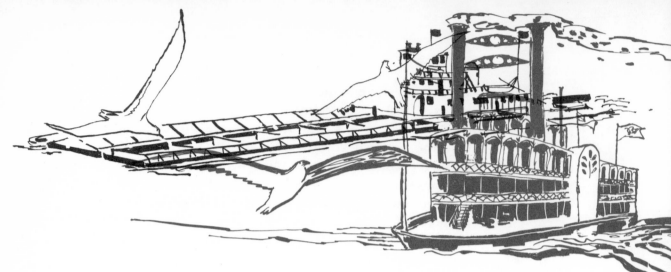

Then came the day of the river steamboat. The sternwheelers and sidewheelers went up and down the Mississippi, the Ohio, and various other rivers—the Cumberland and the Tennessee, the Mobile and the Alabama, and the many navigable streams in Louisiana. New Orleans became a great port. Then roads were built through the wilderness, and stagecoaches traveled where only Indian trails had gone. Finally, railroads came into the South, providing cheap transportation for passengers and freight.

With the coming of highways and railroads, river traffic declined and the channels of many of the streams were allowed to fill up so that they were no longer deep enough for steamboats. It seemed that the colorful day of the waterways was over. But when the TVA built its series of dams, it also installed locks in the dams and deepened the channels of the rivers to nine feet, deep enough for boats. Now the rivers have come into their own again.

The needs of the Second World War increased transportation of freight on the waterways, and with the completion of more dams, river trade continues to grow. Great barges carry millions of tons of freight—cotton and cotton products, steel from Birmingham, farm products, furniture and lumber, and many others—to the Gulf ports and the Gulf Intracoastal Waterway. This wide channel connects all the Gulf ports and all the waterways that empty into the Gulf, from Brownsville, Texas, to Florida. Some of the inland cities have feeder canals that connect with the waterway. Houston, Texas, has built a deep-water ship channel fifty miles long, through which large ships can enter the Houston port.

Ocean-going vessels enter the Mississippi River through New Orleans, now one of the nation's leading seaports, and go to Chicago and the Great Lakes. From there they can go on through the St. Lawrence Seaway to the Atlantic Ocean.

The People

There are many different kinds of people in the Gulf Lands and Central South—Texas cattlemen, Oklahoma Indians, Louisiana Creoles and Cajuns, wealthy plantation owners, sharecroppers and small farmers, businessmen and mountain people, soft-spoken Southerners and brisk Northerners. Each one has his own individuality and each believes that his own particular part of the South is the best there is.

Since the Reconstruction period following the Civil War, there are no slaves and not so many large plantations. Those that are left are still largely worked by Negroes, this time as sharecroppers, and there are white sharecroppers, too, as well as farmers who own their own small farms. Southern traditions and Negro songs and stories and superstitions combine to form the colorful folklore of the South.

The Creoles are descendants of the French and Spanish who lived in southern Louisiana in the early days. They have retained the language and customs of their ancestors. New Orleans is famous for its Creole cooking and other Creole ways of doing things.

The "Cajuns" are French Acadians who were driven out of Nova Scotia, also called Acadia, by the British when they refused to submit to British rule. The Spanish welcomed them to Louisiana. Their flight was made famous by Henry Wadsworth Longfellow's poem, *Evangeline*.

Many mountain people still live in the Great Smokies and other mountains, often in log cabins on small farms that seem to cling to the hillsides. They are the descendants of Scotch and English settlers, and they live isolated lives and carry on the traditions of their ancestors. Many of them still use spinning wheels, weave their own cloth, make their own brooms and furniture and other household articles, and carry their corn to the community's grist mill to be ground into meal. Since modern highways and railroads have penetrated the mountains and brought the outside world closer, the mountain people are beginning to change, too. But handicraft guilds have been formed to encourage them to continue constructing their beautiful handmade furniture, weaving, and other handicrafts, which are eagerly bought by tourists who visit the mountains.

There are more Indians in Oklahoma than in any other state except Arizona, but there are no reservations, for the land was divided among them and each Indian was given his share. Now they live very much as the white people do. Some of them are wealthy, and many are well educated and hold good positions or are professional people, such as doctors or lawyers.

These Indians are the descendants of the Five Civilized Tribes that the government moved to Oklahoma, as well as the Osage Indians and other tribes who already lived in Oklahoma and the Plains Indians who wandered there or who were moved in by the government. Many of them have white blood. Will Rogers was one of the prominent citizens of the state who claimed Indian blood.

The Arts

A love for the fine arts is a significant part of southern culture. Most of the large cities and many of the smaller ones have their symphony orchestras, opera houses, art galleries, and museums, some of which are nationally famous. Spanish and Mexican folksongs from along the Texas border, cowboy songs, and Negro spirituals are all a part of our national folklore. The Indians continue to perform their dances, and the mountain people of Tennessee and Kentucky still sing the English ballads of the Elizabethan Age. New Orleans is credited with being the birthplace of jazz, and her jazz orchestras are world renowned.

The architecture of the South is as varied and interesting as the rest of its culture. Nashville, Tennessee, is often called "the Athens of the South," because of its examples of classical Greek architecture. The Parthenon, used as an art gallery, is an exact replica of the ancient building on the Acropolis at Athens. The architecture of many of the lovely old southern mansions also follows classical traditions.

Nearer the Gulf Coast, we begin to see French and Spanish and Mexican influences. In the old French quarter in New Orleans and in other southern Gulf cities, such as Mobile and Galveston, the houses are often built around courtyards and are trimmed with lacy iron grill-work. In Texas, the influence of the Spanish haciendas, old Spanish missions, and the adobe huts of the Mexicans can be seen. The one-story ranch house, which was developed in Texas, has become popular all over the country.

The cities have their share of skyscrapers, and many of the newer buildings follow the modern lines. Tulsa, Oklahoma, and Dallas, Texas, are especially famous for their many unusual buildings of modern design.

Pioneer homes and their furnishings have been preserved or recon-structed, and Indian artifacts and handiwork are displayed in many museums. An especially fine collection of the work of modern Indian artists is on display in the Philbrook Art Center at Tulsa, Oklahoma.

Much romantic and realistic literature has been written about the South. Sidney Lanier was a famous southern poet. John James Audubon lived in and traveled through the South, painting the birds and mammals of the region and writing about them. Many of his original paintings are on display in the Audubon State Park near Henderson, Kentucky.

Alice Hegan Rice's *Mrs. Wiggs of the Cabbage Patch* and *Lovey Mary* were laid in Kentucky, and so were Annie Fellows Johnston's *Little Colonel* series and *Two Little Knights of Kentucky*. James Lane Allen wrote about Kentucky, and George W. Cable wrote about the Creoles of Louisiana. Booker T. Washington's *Up From Slavery* has become an American classic. The years that O. Henry (whose real name was William Sydney Porter) spent in Texas served as a background for many of his stories.

The stories of Octavus Roy Cohen and Roark Bradford deal largely with the Negroes of the South. The play *The Green Pastures* was adapted from Bradford's *Ol' Man Adam an' His Chillun*. Other southern writers include Irvin S. Cobb, Jesse Stuart, William Faulkner, James Street, J. Frank Dobie, Marquis James, and many others.

Things to think about

Why is this region a huge kingdom of cattle, cotton and oil? Even though these are leading products, why are other crops and minerals important?

How has the Tennessee Valley Authority brought new life and prosperity to the South?

How have waterways influenced the growth of the region from the early days to the present?

Describe the ways of life and the contributions to the region's culture made by the varied peoples of the Gulf Lands—such as the Indians in Oklahoma, the mountain folk in Tennessee and Kentucky, the Texas cattlemen, etc.

Southlands enchantment

The Gulf Lands and Central South is truly a land of enchantment. Never-to-be-forgotten scenery and adventure are to be found in Kentucky's and Tennessee's Cumberland and Great Smoky Mountains, in the Boston and Ouachita Mountains of Arkansas and Oklahoma, in the Arbuckles and Wichitas of Oklahoma, and in the central hill country and the rugged mountains and deep gorges of the trans-Pecos country in Texas. Many of the outstanding scenic points are preserved in state and national parks, such as the Cumberland Falls State Park in Kentucky. This park contains some beautiful waterfalls. On moonlight nights, a lovely moonbow may be seen in the mist of the falls.

Colonial Mansions

It is enchantment just to drive through the countryside and the towns and see the beautiful old colonial mansions, most of them built long before the Civil War. At Natchez, Mississippi, thirty of these old homes are opened to the public in the spring, when the flowers are at their best. In the spring, also, the Azalea Trail Festival is held at Mobile, Alabama, when a tour of seventeen miles is routed past the most beautiful azalea growths and the gardens of homes along the way are open to visitors. The Trail includes the handsome Bellingrath Gardens, with their magnificent camellias, azaleas, gardenias, oleanders, and hundreds of other flowering plants.

Lakes

The great man-made lakes of the South Central and Gulf States have an enchantment all their own. Here are many miles of bathing beaches and water sports of every kind—swimming, fishing, water skiing, water bicycling, sailing, and almost any kind of boating. On some of the lakes are enclosed floating fishing-docks, air-cooled in the summer and heated in the winter. Many a big fish is caught from these docks!

Tennessee has a lake that was made by an earthquake. This is Reelfoot Lake, in the northwest corner of the state. During the Madrid Earthquake of 1811-1812, an area of about fifty-five square miles sank, and the depression filled up with water. Cypress trees grow in the lake, and it is the home of many kinds of water birds, such as egrets, herons, cormorants, anhingas, ducks, and geese.

Historic Shrines

Historic spots are part of the enchantment of the Gulf Lands and Central South. Near Nashville the Hermitage, home of Andrew Jackson, seventh President of the United States, is preserved just as it was when the Jacksons lived in it. The tomb of Jackson and his wife Rachel is on the grounds. The home of James K. Polk, another former President, is at Columbia. Near Bardstown, Kentucky, is "My Old Kentucky Home" State Shrine, the mansion where Stephen Foster is said to have written the famous song. The house and beautifully landscaped grounds are kept as they were when Judge Rowan, cousin of Stephen Foster, lived there. The historic Alamo chapel, where so many brave men died, is preserved at San Antonio, Texas, as a state shrine. All over the South are many other historic shrines.

National Monuments

Many Civil War battlegrounds, burial grounds, and forts are preserved in units of the National Park Service—national historical parks, monuments, sites, and memorials; national military parks and cemeteries; and battlefield parks and sites. The Vicksburg National Military Park and National Cemetery contain the fortifications of the forty-seven-day siege of Vicksburg in 1863 and the cemetery where the soldiers were buried who were killed in the fighting. Pea Ridge National Military Park, established in 1960, was the scene of a great battle fought in Arkansas.

Chickamauga and Chattanooga Military Park, in Tennessee and Georgia, commemorates several important battles fought around Chattanooga. One of these was the famous Battle above the Clouds, fought on Lookout Mountain. Besides the military park, there are some highly scenic rock formations and caves on the mountain. Several thousand fine homes and gardens are in this area. A museum exhibits Civil War relics and Indian artifacts.

Three miles south of Hodgenville, Kentucky, the Abraham Lincoln Birthplace National Historical Site preserves the log cabin where Lincoln was born and the farm, named Sinking Spring, where he spent his first years. The cabin is enclosed in a handsome granite building; leading to it are 56 steps, which represent the 56 years of Lincoln's life.

Cumberland Gap National Historical Park contains the famous gap and two miles of the Wilderness Road, as well as an old mill, a foundry, and Civil War fortifications. It covers more than 20,000 acres in Kentucky, Tennessee, and Virginia, and is highly scenic as well as historic. A high overlook gives sweeping views of surrounding wooded hills and parts of several states in the distance.

The home, tailor shop, and grave of Andrew Johnson, who became President when Lincoln was killed, are preserved in the Andrew Johnson National Monument at Greeneville, Tennessee. Many of the relics of Johnson's day are displayed in the monument.

52

Mammoth Cave National Park

This park contains a series of caverns including the largest and most beautiful cave in Kentucky. It takes about seven hours to go through all of the cave that is open to the public, but this can be divided into several shorter trips. Prehistoric Indians used the cave, and the mummy of one of them can be seen on the Historic Trip, along with sandals and other prehistoric artifacts. Also on the Historic Trip are wooden pipes and vats used to mine saltpeter for making gunpowder during the War of 1812.

There are many other interesting things to see in the cave—wide, spacious corridors and halls, in one of which are towering limestone pillars called the Ruins of Karnak; Echo River, a stream 360 feet below the surface of the earth; Bottomless Pit; Mammoth Dome. At one end of the cave are colorful formations. Stone icicles, called *stalactites,* hang from the ceiling; others, called *stalagmites,* rise from the floor. Huge draperies and other dazzling formations made of stone line the walls. A stone waterfall, called Frozen Niagara, drops for 75 feet.

People visited the cave a hundred years ago and carried lanterns in order to see its wonders. When it became a national park, the Park Service installed electric lights. They also built nature trails outside the cave, where deer, raccoons, squirrels, and other animals may often be seen.

Great Smoky Mountains National Park

This park rides the crest of the Great Smokies on the line between Tennessee and North Carolina, and it contains some of the most beautiful mountains in the Appalachians. They are covered with magnificent forests of evergreen and hardwood, which are a blaze of color in October. Over all hangs a blue haze which gives the mountains their name.

A wide, splendid highway, U.S. 441, crosses the park from Gatlinburg on the Tennessee side to Cherokee, North Carolina. There are other roads, too, one of which goes to Clingmans Dome, highest point in the park. On the mountainsides and along the trails many flowering shrubs and wildflowers bloom in season—redbud, dogwood, mountain laurel, flame azalea, and rhododendron are some of the most showy. Near the park, a blanket of purple rhododendrons covers Roan Mountain in late June.

Some of the mountain cabins of the pioneers who once lived in the park have been preserved so that we can see how these people lived. The Pioneer Farmstead, near the Cherokee entrance, shows the buildings that made up a farm—the log dwelling, barn, meat house, corn crib, and others. A museum nearby exhibits furniture and tools of the pioneers.

On the west side of the park, in Cades Cove, is a small hamlet where the mountain people lived and worked. A few families are still allowed to live here and work the nearby fields, but most of the cabins are empty. An early-day gristmill, operated by a large waterwheel, works from April to October, and the corn meal which it grinds is sold in the nearby Becky Cabie House, where a general store operated for many years. A cane mill makes molasses during the fall months, when the sorghum grass is harvested.

Wild turkeys and deer can sometimes be seen in Cades Cove, especially during the early morning and late evening hours. Bears frequent the roadsides of the park during the summer season and raid the garbage cans. Other animals include red and gray foxes, opossums, raccoons, bobcats, woodchucks, and many more.

Medicinal Springs Parks

Hot Springs National Park is located in Arkansas' Ouachita Mountains. Surrounded by the city of Hot Springs, the park preserves 47 hot springs that are believed to have medicinal values. People suffering from various types of arthritic and rheumatic troubles, nervous tension, and just plain fatigue bathe in the water from these springs, which is available in bathhouses along "Bathhouse Row." People also drink the water. The hot springs were used by the Indians for medicinal purposes

before the coming of the white man. De Soto is believed to be the first white man to discover the springs.

People go to Platt National Park, near Sulphur, Oklahoma, to drink the waters of the cold mineral springs which the park preserves. Some of the springs are bromide and some are sulfur. The park is located in a setting of wooded hills, and two clear streams, with scenic waterfalls, flow through it. Two springs contain pure water, and these are named Buffalo and Antelope because these animals are said to have come here to drink in early days. The Indians frequently came here, also, to drink the medicinal waters.

Big Bend National Park

Located in the big bend of the Rio Grande in Texas, just across the river from Mexico, is one of our most primitive parks. Good roads lead across the park from the north and west entrances to Big Bend's two spectacular canyons, Boquillas on the east, and Santa Elena on the west. A branch road goes to The Basin, in the edge of the Chisos Mountains, where food and lodging are available. But to really see the park, one needs to follow the many horseback trails.

The park is a combination of mountains, castle-like rock formations, spectacular gorges, and deserts. Desert plants and animals prevail, and are more like those found in Mexico than in the United States.

There are more than 1,000 different kinds of plants here, including the giant daggers and other yuccas, the century plant, ocotillo, creosote-bush, catclaws, and various kinds of cactuses. Some of the animals in the park are the coyote, ringtail cat, kit fox, collared peccary, mountain lion, and pronghorn antelope. In the evening, white-tailed deer come down into The Basin to feed, and desert mule deer graze along the park roads.

Things to think about

How is the gracious living, characteristic of the South in by-gone days, being kept alive?

How can many events of the Civil War years be relived today in the South Central United States?

How do areas below the earth's surface provide enchantment?

What special enchantment, characteristic of their locations, can be found in the Great Smokies and in Big Bend National Park?

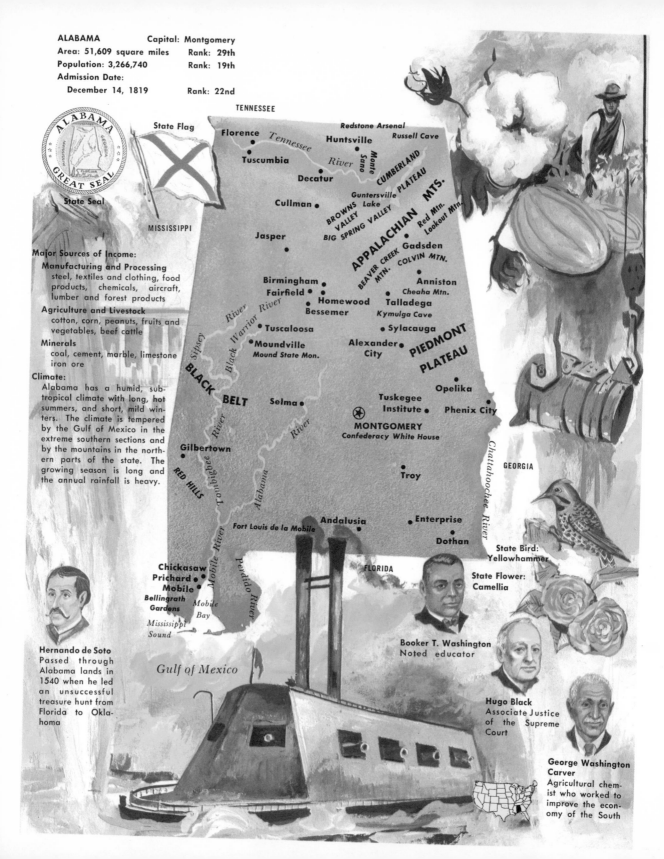

ALABAMA

Area: 51,609 square miles
Population: 3,266,740
Admission Date:
  December 14, 1819

Capital: Montgomery
Rank: 29th
Rank: 19th

Rank: 22nd

State Flag

ALABAMA
GREAT SEAL

State Seal

TENNESSEE

MISSISSIPPI

Major Sources of Income:

Manufacturing and Processing
steel, textiles and clothing, food products, chemicals, aircraft, lumber and forest products

Agriculture and Livestock
cotton, corn, peanuts, fruits and vegetables, beef cattle

Minerals
coal, cement, marble, limestone iron ore

Climate:
Alabama has a humid, subtropical climate with long, hot summers, and short, mild winters. The climate is tempered by the Gulf of Mexico in the extreme southern sections and by the mountains in the northern parts of the state. The growing season is long and the annual rainfall is heavy.

Redstone Arsenal
Florence Tennessee Huntsville Russell Cave
Tuscumbia River Monte Sano
Decatur CUMBERLAND
Guntersville PLATEAU
Cullman Lake BROWNS VALLEY
Jasper BIG SPRING VALLEY APPALACHIAN MTS.
Red Mtn.
Lookout Mtn.
BEAVER CREEK Gadsden
MTN. COLVIN MTN.
Birmingham Anniston
Fairfield Cheaha Mtn.
Homewood Talladega
Bessemer Kymulga Cave
River Sylacauga
Tuscaloosa PIEDMONT
Moundville Alexander
Mound State Mon. City PLATEAU
BLACK Sipsey River Black Warrior River
Opelika
BELT Selma Tuskegee Phenix City
Institute
MONTGOMERY
Confederacy White House
Gilbertown
Troy GEORGIA
RED HILLS Tombigbee River Alabama River River
Chattahoochee River
Andalusia Enterprise
Fort Louis de la Mobile Dothan
Chickasaw FLORIDA
Prichard
Mobile State Bird:
Bellingrath Mobile Yellowhammer
Gardens Bay Perdido River Mobile River
Mississippi State Flower:
Sound Camellia

Gulf of Mexico

Booker T. Washington
Noted educator

Hugo Black
Associate Justice of the Supreme Court

Hernando de Soto
Passed through Alabama lands in 1540 when he led an unsuccessful treasure hunt from Florida to Oklahoma

George Washington Carver
Agricultural chemist who worked to improve the economy of the South

In this state the gracious traditions of the Old South still prevail, and the melodious folk songs of the Negro cotton workers blend with the strident whistle of the factory. Alabama was one of the first southern states to welcome the invasion of heavy industry. Nowhere else in the world are coal, iron, and limestone, the three minerals necessary for making steel, found so close together as they are in Alabama. In Birmingham and Gadsden, great blast furnaces produce the steel that other factories make into machinery and tools and many other things needed in the nation's economy.

Important Whens and Whats in the Making of Alabama

1528 Spanish conquistador Pánfilo de Narváez explores inland in search of gold.

1540 Hernando de Soto leads another unsuccessful treasure hunt through Alabama lands.

1682 La Salle claims the land for France.

1702 The French, under Bienville, establish a colony at Mobile.

1763 All French land east of the Mississippi River is ceded to England.

1783 England cedes the land to the United States after the Revolutionary War.

1814 Settlement becomes heavy after the defeat of the Creek Indians.

1817 The Alabama Territory is created.

1819 Alabama is admitted to the Union as the 22nd state.

1861 Alabama secedes from the Union and joins the Confederacy.

1868 Alabama is readmitted to the Union.

Alabama has hundreds of miles of navigable streams, and the state is constructing inland river docks throughout her river system. The Mobile-Tombigbee-Warrior Waterway connects Birmingham with Mobile Bay and the Intracoastal Waterway system. The Chattahoochee River, which forms part of the boundary with Georgia, is also being deepened for barge travel.

The numerous dams which have been built on the rivers of the state not only aid in flood control and furnish low-cost power to the increasing number of factories, they also aid navigation. During flood time, they back up the surplus water into large lakes. Then, when the rivers shrink during the summer and fall months, the dams release enough water into the streams to keep them navigable.

The Tennessee River flows down from Tennessee's mountains into Alabama and makes a great arc across the northern end of the state before turning again across Tennessee and Kentucky into the Ohio River. Millions of tons of northern Alabama's agricultural and industrial products pass through the locks of the great TVA dams each year and go to cities in the Ohio and upper Mississippi valleys. Other millions of tons of products, such as automobiles and grain from the Midwest and coal from Kentucky, come to the South. The lakes also serve as recreational areas, with fine fishing, boating, and swimming.

The flags of five nations have flown over Alabama. De Soto raised the Spanish flag over the area when he explored it in 1540, but Spain could not hold the region against the French, who claimed it as a result of La Salle's later explorations. France lost it to England in 1763, and it came into the possession of the new American nation at the end of the Revolutionary War. After being admitted to the Union in 1819, Alabama was one of the first states to secede, and for four years the flag of the Confederacy flew over her. Following the Civil War, the bitter days of the Reconstruction period took heavy toll of Alabama's resources. Since that time, however, the state has made rapid progress in her return to prosperity.

ARKANSAS
Area: 53,104 square miles
Population: 1,786,272
Admission Date: June 15, 1836

Capital: Little Rock
Rank: 27th
Rank: 31st
Rank: 25th

State Seal

State Flower:
Apple Blossom

State Flag

State Bird:
Mockingbird

MISSOURI

OZARK   PLATEAU
Bull Shoals Res.
Lake Norfolk
Springdale   Harrison
Marble Falls
Fayetteville
Batesville

Boston Mountains
Arkansas River   Medicinal Springs

Fort Smith   Russelville

OKLAHOMA
Poteau   Magazine Mtn.
Mtn.
Petit Jean Mtn.   Nimrod Res.
Ouachita   Mountains   Jacksonville
Muddy Creek
Mtn.   Hot Springs Nat'l Park
Blue Mtn.   Hot Springs
Lake
Ouachita   Lake
Catherine   Benton
Caddo Mts.
Cossatot Mts.
Cross Mts.

Murfreesboro
Crater of Diamonds
Hope
Camden   Ouachita River

TEXAS
Texarkana   Red River   Magnolia

El Dorado

LOUISIANA

Black River
Ridge
Paragould   Blytheville
Jonesboro
St. Francis River
Crowleys

Ozark   St. Francis Basin   PLAIN
Escarpment
West
Memphis
White   Forrest
City
River   TENNESSEE

LITTLE ROCK   COASTAL   Helena   MISSISSIPPI

Stuttgart
Arkansas
River   Pine Bluff
Arkansas
Post   GULF
MISSISSIPPI   RIVER

**Douglas
MacArthur**
Army general and
liberator of the
Philippines during
World War II;
born at Little Rock

Hernando de Soto
Led the first white
men into the Ar-
kansas region in
1541-1542

Major Sources of Income:
   Agriculture and Livestock
      cotton, soybeans, rice, hay, corn, oats, fruits and
      vegetables, cattle, hogs and sheep, poultry and dairy
      products
   Manufacturing and Processing
      food products, lumber, wood, pulp and paper prod-
      ucts, furniture, chemicals, textiles and clothing
   Forestry
      pine, oak
   Minerals
      petroleum, natural gas, bauxite, sand and gravel,
      stone
   Climate:
      Arkansas' climate is generally humid and subtropical
      with long, hot summers and short, mild winters. Tem-
      peratures seldom go below freezing but some snow
      falls in the mountains. There is an abundant annual
      rainfall of almost 50 inches.

The topography of Arkansas is divided sharply into two sections. The northwest section, extending eastward to the Black River, is occupied by the Ozark Plateau and the Boston Mountains and, farther south, by the Ouachita Mountains. The Ouachitas are separated from the Boston Mountains by the upper Arkansas River Valley. The rest of the state is made up of lowlands, with the broad, fertile Mississippi flood plain in the east and the Gulf Coastal Plain in the south.

Important Whens and Whats in the Making of Arkansas

1541-1542 Hernando de Soto leads the first white men into the Arkansas region.

1673 Frenchmen Marquette and Jolliet reach the mouth of the Arkansas River.

1682 La Salle claims the land for France.

1686 The French establish a trading post settlement at Arkansas Post.

1763 With other French territory west of the Mississippi River, the region is ceded to Spain.

1800 The region is regained by France.

1803 Arkansas land is included in the territory sold to the United States by the Louisiana Purchase.

1818 A cotton boom brings many settlers to the Arkansas region.

1819 The Arkansas Territory is created.

1836 Arkansas is admitted to the Union as the 25th state.

1861 Seceding from the Union, Arkansas joins the Confederacy.

1868 Arkansas is readmitted to the Union.

Arkansas' many rivers drain into the Mississippi. The Arkansas River enters the state from Oklahoma on the west and flows southeastward across the state to the Mississippi, while the White and the St. Francis come down from Missouri on the north. The Red River cuts across the corner of the state into Louisiana, and forms part of the line between Arkansas and Texas. The Ouachita River and its tributaries drain south-central Arkansas before entering Louisiana. The state also has many natural and man-made lakes, with several oxbow lakes, such as Lake Chicot, along the Mississippi River.

Two of Arkansas' most important agricultural products are cotton, grown over most of the state, and rice, which is found in the irrigated section between the lower Arkansas and White rivers. During its growth, rice must be covered with six inches or more of water, and this section of the Mississippi flood plain, with its many bayous, or small streams, is ideal for this purpose. Level fields, or paddies, are surrounded with earthen dikes, which keep the water at the proper level. When the grain ripens, the paddies are drained by means of sluice gates so that heavy machinery can get in to harvest the crop.

Every year many tourists visit Arkansas' highly scenic Ozark and Ouachita mountains, Hot Springs National Park, and the nearby string of man-made lakes—Catherine, Hamilton, and Ouachita. Bull Shoals Reservoir and Lake Norfork are also popular recreation areas. Fascinating caves, interesting towns, and national forests are additional tourist attractions.

The town of Calico Rock, south of Lake Norfork, is built on three levels. It gets its name from a high bluff that is marked with brightly-colored stripes, checks, and squares, like a calico print. Eureka Springs, near the northwest corner of the state, clings to the steep slope of an Ozark mountain, and its streets run up and down and around the mountain. It contains many mineral springs and is one of Arkansas' oldest tourist resorts. Pea Ridge Battlefield is nearby.

The bauxite open-pit, or "strip," mines, southwest of Little Rock, are of interest to visitors, and so is the diamond mine near Murfreesboro. At this mine, which is no longer worked commercially, guests are allowed to hunt for diamonds and are given free all they find that are not over five carats.

Arkansas, like most of the other South Central and Gulf States, was in the possession of several sovereign powers at various times. The area was first explored by De Soto, and later claimed by France on the basis of La Salle's trip down the Mississippi. France gave the land to Spain in 1763, reclaimed it in 1800, and sold it to the United States in 1803. The flag of the Confederacy flew over it during the four years of the Civil War, and several important battles were fought on its soil.

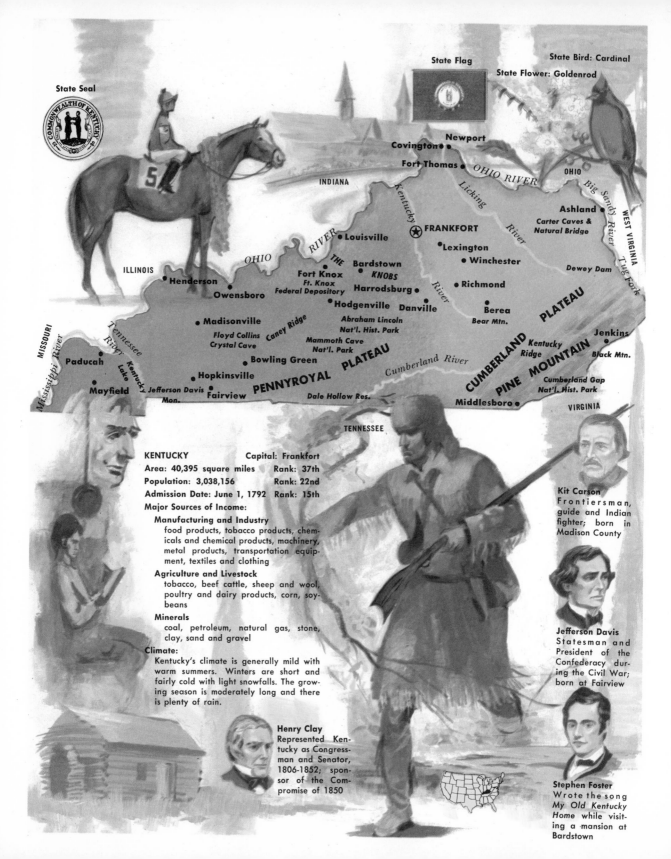

State Seal

State Flag

State Bird: Cardinal

State Flower: Goldenrod

INDIANA

ILLINOIS

MISSOURI

OHIO

WEST VIRGINIA

VIRGINIA

TENNESSEE

Newport
Covington
Fort Thomas
OHIO RIVER
Kentucky River
FRANKFORT
Licking River
Ashland
Carter Caves &
Natural Bridge

OHIO RIVER
Louisville
Lexington
Winchester
THE
Bardstown
KNOBS
Fort Knox
Ft. Knox
Federal Depository
Harrodsburg
Richmond
Dewey Dam

Henderson
Owensboro
Hodgenville
Danville
Berea
Bear Mtn.
CUMBERLAND PLATEAU
Jenkins
Black Mtn.

Madisonville
Floyd Collins
Crystal Cave
Caney Ridge
Abraham Lincoln
Nat'l. Hist. Park
Mammoth Cave
Nat'l. Park
Kentucky Ridge
PINE MOUNTAIN

Paducah
Tennessee River
Kentucky Lake
Bowling Green
Cumberland River
Cumberland Gap
Nat'l. Hist. Park

Mayfield
Hopkinsville
Jefferson Davis
Mon.
Fairview
Dale Hollow Res.
Middlesboro

Mississippi River

PENNYROYAL PLATEAU

TENNESSEE

KENTUCKY   Capital: Frankfort
Area: 40,395 square miles   Rank: 37th
Population: 3,038,156   Rank: 22nd
Admission Date: June 1, 1792 Rank: 15th
Major Sources of Income:

Manufacturing and Industry
food products, tobacco products, chemicals and chemical products, machinery,
metal products, transportation equipment, textiles and clothing

Agriculture and Livestock
tobacco, beef cattle, sheep and wool,
poultry and dairy products, corn, soybeans

Minerals
coal, petroleum, natural gas, stone,
clay, sand and gravel

Climate:
Kentucky's climate is generally mild with
warm summers. Winters are short and
fairly cold with light snowfalls. The growing season is moderately long and there
is plenty of rain.

Kit Carson
Frontiersman,
guide and Indian
fighter; born in
Madison County

Jefferson Davis
Statesman and
President of the
Confederacy dur-
ing the Civil War;
born at Fairview

Henry Clay
Represented Ken-
tucky as Congress-
man and Senator,
1806-1852; spon-
sor of the Com-
promise of 1850

Stephen Foster
Wrote the song
My Old Kentucky
Home while visit-
ing a mansion at
Bardstown

Kentucky, the "Bluegrass State," received its nickname from the gently rolling north-central Bluegrass Region. This area, whose fertile soil is underlaid with limestone, is the home of the Thoroughbred horse, for which the state is well known. The internationally famous horse race, the Kentucky Derby, is run every May at Louisville's Churchill Downs.

Southwest of the Bluegrass Region and separated from it by an area of low hills called the Knobs is another gently rolling section known as the Pennyroyal, which surrounds the Western Coal Field on three sides. The extreme southwest corner of the state is called the Purchase, because it was bought from the Indians. In this area, a loop of the Mississippi River separates a small section of land from the rest of the state, and it can be reached only by going through Missouri or Tennessee. The Mountain Region occupies eastern Kentucky; it is also called the Eastern Coal Field because so much coal is mined there.

Important Whens and Whats in the Making of Kentucky

1763 At the end of the French and Indian War, French claims east of the Mississippi River, including Kentucky lands, are ceded to England.

1769-1771 Daniel Boone and others explore parts of the Kentucky region.

1774 Captain James Harrod's surveying party lays out Harrodstown, now Harrodsburg.

1775 A party of pioneers, led by Daniel Boone, settles Boonesboro.

1776 Originally part of Virginia's Fincastle County, the land becomes Kentucky County, Virginia.

1780 Louisville is founded at the falls of the Ohio River.

1792 Kentucky is admitted to the Union as the 15th state.

Kentucky's manufacturing centers are largely along the Ohio River. An important transportation route, the river forms the state's northern border and separates it from Ohio, Indiana, and Illinois.

Tobacco is Kentucky's most important agricultural product.

Kentucky, with its southern traditions and lovely old colonial homes, is rich in historic lore. Early settlers came down the Ohio and Kentucky rivers or followed Daniel Boone through the Cumberland Gap. At Harrodsburg, the state's oldest town, the Pioneer Memorial State Park contains a log replica of the old Fort Harrod stockade and block-houses which surround some pioneer cabins and Kentucky's first school-house. Here, also, is the Lincoln Marriage Temple, which shelters the cabin where Lincoln's parents were married. Daniel and Rebecca Boone are buried at Frankfort. The Federal Gold Depository is at Fort Knox.

Abraham Lincoln, the nation's Civil War President, and Jefferson Davis, President of the Confederacy during the four years of its existence, were both born in Kentucky. Lincoln's birthplace and other historic sites connected with the Lincoln family are preserved in national and state parks. On the site of Davis' birthplace, in the Davis Memorial Park at Fairview, a concrete monument, 351 feet high, has been erected to the memory of the Confederacy President. Nearby is a reproduction of the two-room log cabin in which he was born. Kentucky did not secede from the Union, but there were many Southern sympathizers in the state, and some important battles were fought on her soil.

Because of its historic and scenic attractions, the state has a big tourist trade. Mammoth Cave with its spectacular onyx cave formations, and other caverns, hollowed out of the soft limestone by underground water, attract many visitors. Other popular recreation areas are the man-made lakes—Cumberland and Herrington, as well as Dale Hollow and the immense Kentucky Lake, both of which are shared with Tennessee.

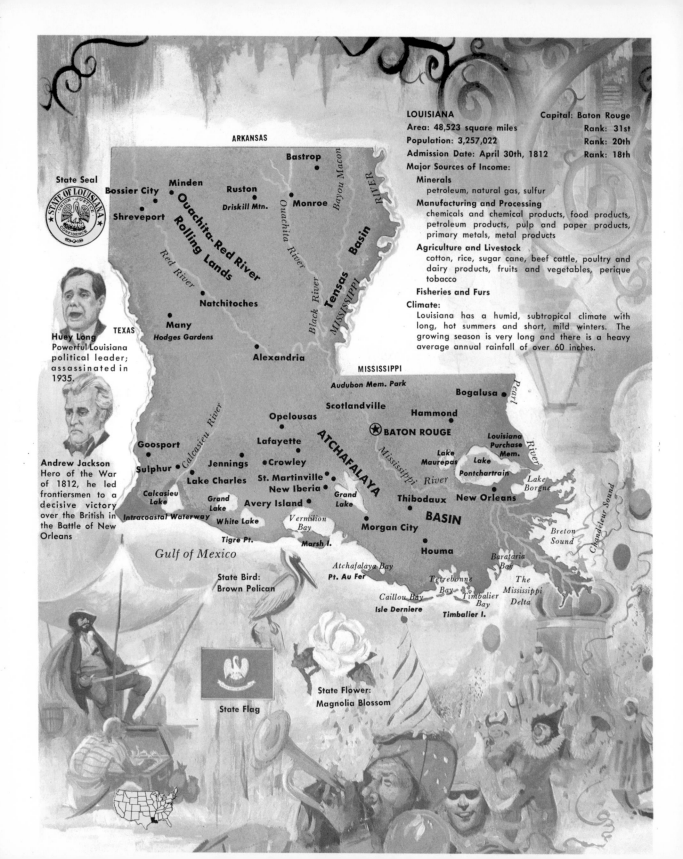

ARKANSAS

LOUISIANA

Area: 48,523 square miles   Capital: Baton Rouge

Population: 3,257,022   Rank: 31st

Admission Date: April 30th, 1812   Rank: 20th

   Rank: 18th

Major Sources of Income:

   Minerals
     petroleum, natural gas, sulfur

   Manufacturing and Processing
     chemicals and chemical products, food products, petroleum products, pulp and paper products, primary metals, metal products

   Agriculture and Livestock
     cotton, rice, sugar cane, beef cattle, poultry and dairy products, fruits and vegetables, perique tobacco

   Fisheries and Furs

Climate:
   Louisiana has a humid, subtropical climate with long, hot summers and short, mild winters. The growing season is very long and there is a heavy average annual rainfall of over 60 inches.

State Seal

STATE OF LOUISIANA
UNION · JUSTICE
CONFIDENCE

TEXAS

Huey Long
Powerful Louisiana political leader; assassinated in 1935.

Andrew Jackson
Hero of the War of 1812, he led frontiersmen to a decisive victory over the British in the Battle of New Orleans

Bastrop

Bayou Macon

RIVER

Minden

Bossier City

Ruston

Driskill Mtn.

Monroe

Shreveport

Ouachita-Red River Rolling Lands

Ouachita River

MISSISSIPPI

Tensas Basin

Red River

Black River

Natchitoches

Many

Hodges Gardens

Alexandria

MISSISSIPPI

Audubon Mem. Park

Scotlandville

Opelousas

Hammond

Bogalusa

Pearl

Calcasieu River

Lafayette

ATCHAFALAYA

★ BATON ROUGE

Louisiana Purchase Mem.

River

Goosport

Sulphur

Jennings

Crowley

Lake Maurepas

Lake Pontchartrain

Lake Borgne

Lake Charles

St. Martinville

New Iberia

Mississippi River

Calcasieu Lake

Grand Lake

Avery Island

Grand Lake

Thibodaux

New Orleans

Intracoastal Waterway

White Lake

Vermilion Bay

BASIN

Chandeleur Sound

Tigre Pt.

Marsh I.

Morgan City

Houma

Breton Sound

Gulf of Mexico

State Bird: Brown Pelican

Atchafalaya Bay

Pt. Au Fer

Barataria Bay

Caillou Bay

Tetrebonne Bay

Timbalier Bay

The Mississippi Delta

Isle Derniere

Timbalier I.

State Flower: Magnolia Blossom

State Flag

Shaped like a giant boot, Louisiana lies with the full length of the "foot" bordering the Gulf of Mexico. The Sabine River and lake separate the "heel" from Texas, and the top of the boot is formed by the Arkansas boundary. The Mississippi River forms the front of the boot and then penetrates the "toe" to the very tip, which ends in the Mississippi Delta.

Important Whens and Whats in the Making of Louisiana

1528 Less than ten years after Alvarez de Pineda came to the region, another Spanish explorer, Cabeza de Vaca, visits the land.

1541 Hernando de Soto explores the region.

1682 La Salle claims the land for France.

1714 The French build Fort St. Jean Baptiste, which later becomes the city of Natchitoches.

1718 New Orleans is founded.

1731 Louisiana becomes a French colony.

1763 Land west of the Mississippi River is ceded to Spain and England receives the land east of the Mississippi.

1800 Spanish Louisiana is returned to France.

1803 With the Louisiana Purchase, the United States receives French holdings, including part of Louisiana; settlement of the West Florida controversy extends United States territory and the Territory of Orleans is created.

1812 Louisiana is admitted to the Union as the 18th state.

1815 American forces led by General Andrew Jackson defeat the British in the Battle of New Orleans.

1861 Louisiana secedes from the Union and joins the Confederacy.

1868 Louisiana is readmitted to the Union.

71

The state has 6,000 miles of rivers and bayous, and the Intracoastal Waterway runs the full length of her coast line and intersects the Mississippi. As a result, Louisiana has long been an important shipping center, and she now has three deep-water ports—New Orleans, Baton Rouge, and Lake Charles. The great port of New Orleans, on the Mississippi and the Gulf of Mexico, has trade routes all over the world. Baton Rouge, at the head of deep-water navigation on the Mississippi, is a point of transfer between deep-sea ships and shallow-water barges. Lake Charles, a growing port in the "heel of the boot," is connected with the Intracoastal Waterway by a ship canal.

Louisiana is unique in the number of special resources and products that she excels in. With oil reserves under practically the whole state and under the water bordering her coast line as well, she claims second place in the production of petroleum. She also holds second place in both the production of natural gas and of sulfur, and third place in the production of salt. She grows much of the nation's sugar cane, and is one of the leading states in the cultivation of rice. And she is the only state in the Union that can grow the strong, dark, highly specialized tobacco known as perique. Cotton, however, is still her most important crop.

Louisiana's fisheries lead in the production of shrimps, oysters, and frogs. More muskrats are trapped in her marshlands and bayou areas than in any other state.

The state's thousands of miles of inland rivers and coast line are not an unmixed blessing, for hurricanes from the sea and flooding rivers sometimes cause great damage and loss of life. High levees have raised the banks of the Mississippi above the surrounding countryside, and these levees must be constantly inspected and repaired to prevent disastrous floods.

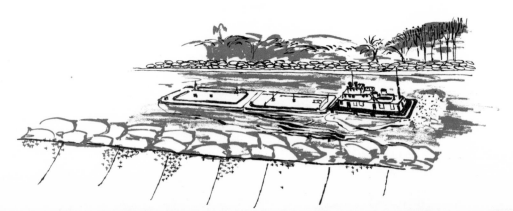

Although Louisiana, like the other southern states, has advanced rapidly in industrial growth, she still retains much of her Old World flavor. There are many historic old buildings and other landmarks at Natchitoches and throughout the state. New Orleans is famous for its Vieux Carré, or Old French Quarter, with its Creole homes built around courtyards and its historic French Market. In another section of the city is the Garden District, where wealthy American settlers built their homes. The Mardi Gras, internationally famed festival, is held in New Orleans each year, preceding Lent.

The René Beauregard House, built in 1840, stands on the site of the famous Battle of New Orleans in the War of 1812. Won by the American forces under Andrew Jackson, the battle was fought fifteen days after the war was over, because communication was so slow at that time that the combatants did not know peace had been declared. The house now contains a battle museum.

Another famous old home is the Shadows on the Teche, which stands beside the Bayou Teche in New Iberia. During the Civil War when Louisiana was a member of the Confederacy, the house was occupied by a Federal general. It is now open to the public.

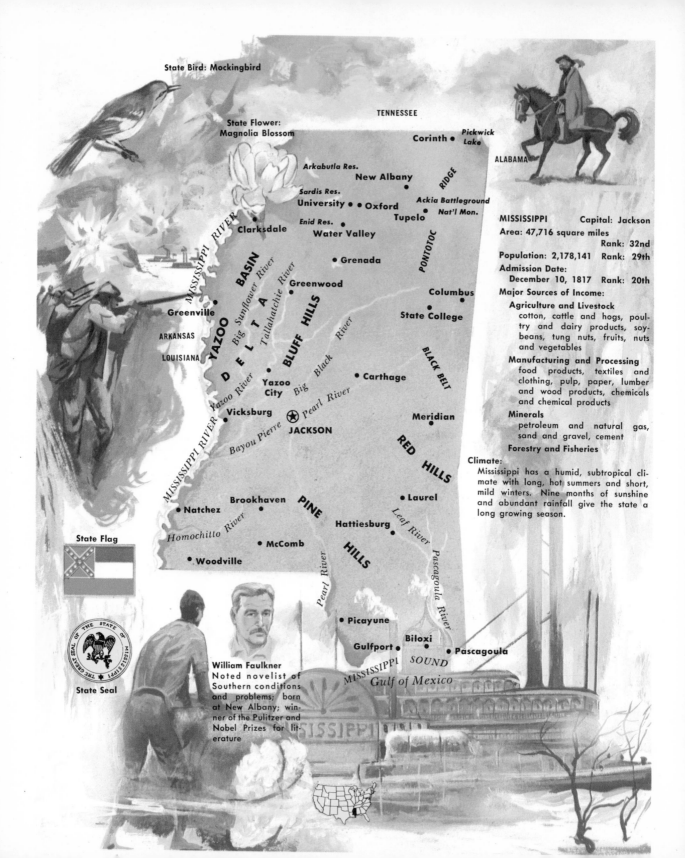

State Bird: Mockingbird

TENNESSEE

Corinth

Pickwick Lake

ALABAMA

State Flower: Magnolia Blossom

Arkabutla Res.

New Albany

RIDGE

Sardis Res.

University • Oxford

Ackia Battleground Nat'l Mon.

Tupelo

Enid Res.

Clarksdale

Water Valley

MISSISSIPPI RIVER

PONTOTOC

Grenada

YAZOO BASIN

Big Sunflower River

Tallahatchie River

Greenwood

DELTA

BLUFF HILLS

Columbus

State College

Greenville

ARKANSAS

LOUISIANA

Yazoo River

Big Black River

BLACK BELT

Carthage

Yazoo City

Vicksburg

Bayou Pierre

Pearl River

JACKSON

Meridian

MISSISSIPPI RIVER

RED HILLS

Natchez

Brookhaven

PINE

Laurel

Homochitto River

McComb

HILLS

Hattiesburg

Leaf River

Pascagoula River

Woodville

Pearl River

Picayune

Gulfport

Biloxi

Pascagoula

MISSISSIPPI SOUND

Gulf of Mexico

MISSISSIPPI

MISSISSIPPI   Capital: Jackson

Area: 47,716 square miles

        Rank: 32nd

Population: 2,178,141   Rank: 29th

Admission Date:

    December 10, 1817   Rank: 20th

Major Sources of Income:

  Agriculture and Livestock
    cotton, cattle and hogs, poultry and dairy products, soybeans, tung nuts, fruits, nuts and vegetables

  Manufacturing and Processing
    food products, textiles and clothing, pulp, paper, lumber and wood products, chemicals and chemical products

  Minerals
    petroleum and natural gas, sand and gravel, cement

  Forestry and Fisheries

Climate:
    Mississippi has a humid, subtropical climate with long, hot summers and short, mild winters. Nine months of sunshine and abundant rainfall give the state a long growing season.

State Flag

State Seal

William Faulkner
Noted novelist of Southern conditions and problems; born at New Albany; winner of the Pulitzer and Nobel Prizes for literature

Mississippi combines the spell of the Old South with the industrial New South. Magnolias, moss-hung live oaks, and beautiful old mansions built before the Civil War bring back memories of great cotton plantations, with their traditions of gracious living. Today gracious living still prevails, although many of the plantations have been broken up into smaller farms.

Southeastern Mississippi borders the Gulf of Mexico, and her miles of clean, white bathing beaches are popular with tourists and home folks alike. Biloxi and Gulfport are important seaports as well as bases for the shrimp and oyster fleets. Beauvoir, the home of Jefferson Davis, President of the Confederacy, is at Biloxi.

Important Whens and Whats in the Making of Mississippi

1540   De Soto crosses the region in search of gold.

1699   The French, under Iberville, make the first settlement at Biloxi Bay.

1763   The French lose all claims east of the Mississippi River to England.

1779   Spain gains control of the region.

1798   The United States takes over the region and creates the Territory of Mississippi which includes what is now Alabama.

1817   Mississippi is admitted to the Union as the 20th state.

1861   A large plantation state, Mississippi is the second state to secede from the Union and join the Confederacy.

1863   Vicksburg falls to Union forces.

1870   Mississippi is readmitted to the Union.

Several large, man-made lakes—the Arkabutla, Sardis, Enid, and Granada—provide power for the state's growing industries. Pickwick Lake forms the state's extreme northeastern corner. Mississippi has taken full advantage of her newly acquired industial power with her plan to "Balance Agriculture with Industry," called the BAWI for short. This program allows a political unit, such as a city or county, to attract manufacturing industries by making suitable land and buildings available to them. The program has resulted in many factories that process the state's agricultural and forest products.

The meandering Mississippi River forms most of the state's west border. In places the river has cut across its loops, making oxbow lakes, and occasionally leaving small portions of Arkansas, Louisiana, and Mississippi on the wrong side of the river. The area between the Mississippi and the Yazoo, called "the Delta" by the natives, contains some of the richest soil in Mississippi. Here the long-staple variety of cotton, for which the state is famous, is grown. Another important river is the Pearl, which comes down through the center of the state and forms the boundary along the southeast portion of Louisiana.

The flags of France, England, Spain, the United States, and the southern Confederacy have flown over Mississippi. The state seceded from the Union on January 9, 1861, and several great battles of the Civil War were fought on her soil, culminating in the Siege of Vicksburg. The surrender of the city on July 4, 1863, was an important turning point in the war.

The Natchez Trace Parkway, now a unit of the National Park Service, starts at Natchez and crosses the corner of Alabama to Nashville, Tennessee. It was once a heavily traveled Indian trail, and later was used by pioneers who floated their products down the Mississippi River on flatboats and then returned home on foot.

77

State Flag

State Seal

OKLAHOMA

State Bird:
Scissor-tailed Flycatcher

COLORADO

KANSAS

MISSOURI

NEW MEXICO

Black Mesa
Kenton
Dinosaur Quarry

North Canadian River

Freedom
Great Salt
Plains Res.
Alabaster Caverns

Ponca City

Bartlesville

Miami

OZARK
PLATEAU

TEXAS

Cimarron River

Fort Supply Res.

Enid

Will Rogers Mem.
Claremore

Stillwater

Tulsa

Canton Res.

Canadian

Arkansas

Sapulpa

BOSTON
MTNS.

State Flower:
Mistletoe

El Reno

River

OKLAHOMA CITY

Muskogee

OKLAHOMA   Capital: Oklahoma City

Area: 69,919 square miles   Rank: 18th

Population: 2,328,284   Rank: 27th

Admission Date:
November 16, 1907   Rank: 46th

Major Sources of Income:

Minerals
petroleum, natural gas, cement, zinc,
lead, coal

Manufacturing and Processing
food products, petroleum and coal
products, machinery, transportation
equipment, stone, clay and glass products

Agriculture and Livestock
wheat, cotton, corn, small grains, cattle
and hogs, dairy and poultry products,
fruits, nuts, and vegetables

Climate:
Eastern Oklahoma has plenty of rainfall
and is like the humid, subtropical southeastern parts of the nation. The western
part of the state is like the dry western
sections of the country. Oklahoma's panhandle receives little rain and is sometimes subject to drought and "dust bowl"
conditions. Temperatures range from below freezing in the winter to more than
100 degrees in the summer. The growing season ranges from a moderate 180
days in the panhandle to a long 240
days in the southeastern sections.

Shawnee

Okmulgee

River

Indian City U.S.A.

Midwest
City

North Canadian River

Rainy Mtn.

Anadarko

Seminole

Altus

Wichita Mtns.

Southern Plains Ind.
Arts & Crafts Mus.

Ada

McAlester

Lawton

Wichita Mtns.
Nat'l Wildlife Ref.   Duncan

Platt Nat'l Park

Arbuckle Mts.

Tuskahoma   Mtn.

Kiamichi

OUACHITA
MOUNTAINS

Ardmore

Tishomingo
Lake Texoma

Durant

Ouachita
Nat'l Forest

RED   RIVER

Denison Dam

RED   RIVER

ARKANSAS

TEXAS

Maria Tallchief
Great American
classic ballerina;
born at Fairfax,
the daughter of
an Osage Indian
chief

Will Rogers
Cowboy, philos-
opher and humor-
ist; born near
Claremore

Jim Thorpe
One of America's
greatest athletes;
born at Prague

Oklahoma, once considered dry and barren and fit only for the Indians, is now one of the richest states in the Union, due to scientific methods of farming and to the discovery of petroleum and natural gas. Some of the Indians, on whose tribal lands oil was found, are among the wealthiest people in the United States.

The state is largely a plains area, rising from the grassy prairies in the eastern and central portions to the High Plains of the west. The Ozark Plateau extends into eastern Oklahoma from Arkansas, and, farther south, the Ouachita Mountains also enter the state. To the west are the low Arbuckles and Wichitas.

Important Whens and Whats in the Making of Oklahoma

1541   Spanish explorer Coronado crosses the area in search of gold.

1542   De Soto explores along the eastern edge of the region.

1682   La Salle claims the area for France.

1763   France cedes the region with other land to Spain.

1802   After regaining the region, the French make the first white settlement at Salina.

1803   The Oklahoma region is sold to the United States with other land in the Lousiana Purchase.

1825   Part of the region is set aside for the Five Civilized Tribes and is known as Indian Territory.

1889   Oklahoma's first oil well is drilled at Chelsea; part of the land is opened to settlement with the first land "run."

1890   The land opened by the run is organized as Oklahoma Territory.

1905   Glenn Pool, Oklahoma's first large oil field, is discovered.

1907   Oklahoma, including Indian Territory, is admitted to the Union as the 46th state.

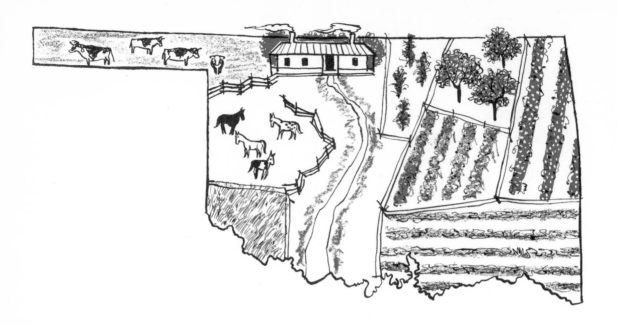

In the eastern part of Oklahoma, crops typical of the Midwest, such as corn and small grains, mingle with cotton, pecans, peanuts, and other southern crops. The drier west is largely devoted to cattle ranches, and the growing of sorghum, grains, and winter wheat.

Two of Oklahoma's largest rivers, the Cimarron and the Canadian, with their tributaries, flow eastward across the state into the Arkansas River, which cuts across the northeast corner into Arkansas and eventually empties into the Mississippi. Other streams flow southward into the Red River, which forms the boundary with Texas and enters the Mississippi in Louisiana. Large man-made lakes include Grand Lake of the Cherokees, and Fort Gibson and Tenkiller lakes along the western slope of the Ozark Plateau. Huge Lake Texoma is on the Texas border.

Oklahoma has done much to attract a growing tourist trade and make good its boast, "You'll have the time of your life in Oklahoma." Fine state parks have been established in many sections, and there are comfortable living accommodations and facilities for having fun. Pioneer relics and Indian artifacts have been preserved in museums all over the state and the Indians are encouraged to keep alive their traditional dances and ceremonials.

South of Lake Fort Gibson are the Fort Gibson Stockade, built in 1824 and carefully reconstructed by the state, and Fort Gibson National Cemetery. The Will Rogers Memorial, near Claremore, contains the tomb of the famous humorist and philosopher, as well as a museum which displays many of his personal effects. The cabin of Sequoyah, inventor of the Cherokee alphabet, is preserved as a national shrine near the Arkansas state line. The National Cowboy Hall of Fame and Museum is at Oklahoma City. In the Wichita Mountains National Wildlife Refuge are buffalo, elk, deer, antelope, longhorn cattle, and other animals, as well as a large recreation area. Anadarko has the Southern Plains Indian Arts and Crafts Museum; nearby is Indian City U.S.A., with faithfully reconstructed Indian villages and museum. These are only a few of the attractions that are making the tourist trade almost as important in Oklahoma as petroleum and agriculture.

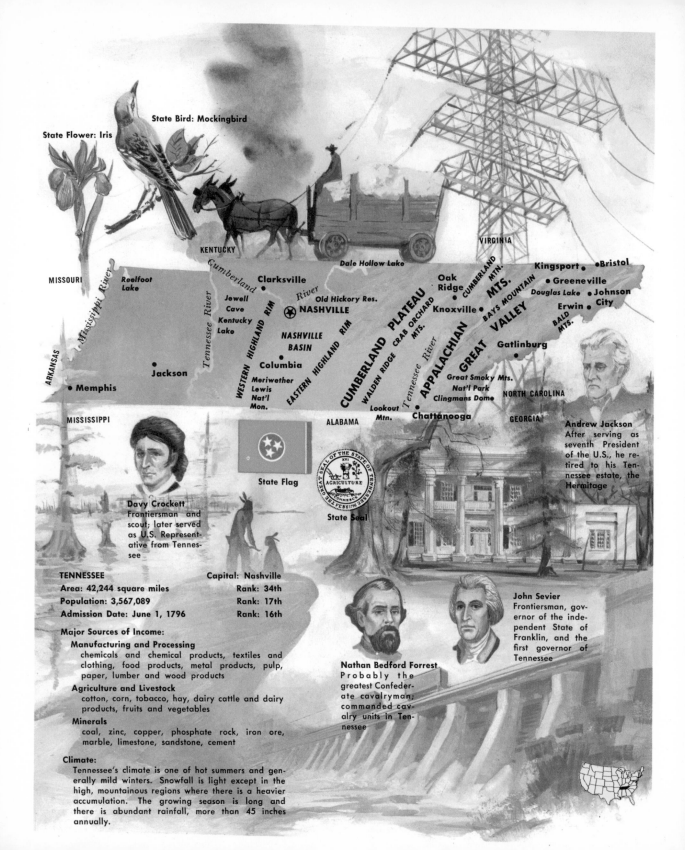

State Flower: Iris

State Bird: Mockingbird

KENTUCKY

VIRGINIA

MISSOURI

Mississippi River

Cumberland River

Dale Hollow Lake

Reelfoot Lake

Clarksville

Old Hickory Res.

Kingsport • Bristol

Oak Ridge

CUMBERLAND MTN.

• Greeneville

Tennessee River

Jewell Cave

NASHVILLE

CUMBERLAND PLATEAU

Knoxville

Douglas Lake

Johnson City

Kentucky Lake

NASHVILLE BASIN

CRAB ORCHARD MTS.

BAYS MOUNTAIN

GREAT VALLEY

Erwin

ARKANSAS

WESTERN HIGHLAND RIM

EASTERN HIGHLAND RIM

WALDEN RIDGE

APPALACHIAN MTS.

BALD MTS.

Columbia

Gatlinburg

Jackson

Meriwether Lewis Nat'l Mon.

Tennessee River

Great Smoky Mts. Nat'l Park
Clingmans Dome

NORTH CAROLINA

• Memphis

Lookout Mtn.

Chattanooga

MISSISSIPPI

ALABAMA

GEORGIA

State Flag

GREAT SEAL OF THE STATE OF TENNESSEE
AGRICULTURE
COMMERCE
1796 FEB 6 XVI

State Seal

Andrew Jackson
After serving as seventh President of the U.S., he retired to his Tennessee estate, the Hermitage

Davy Crockett
Frontiersman and scout; later served as U.S. Representative from Tennessee

TENNESSEE
Area: 42,244 square miles
Population: 3,567,089
Admission Date: June 1, 1796

Capital: Nashville
Rank: 34th
Rank: 17th
Rank: 16th

Major Sources of Income:

Manufacturing and Processing
chemicals and chemical products, textiles and clothing, food products, metal products, pulp, paper, lumber and wood products

Agriculture and Livestock
cotton, corn, tobacco, hay, dairy cattle and dairy products, fruits and vegetables

Minerals
coal, zinc, copper, phosphate rock, iron ore, marble, limestone, sandstone, cement

Climate:
Tennessee's climate is one of hot summers and generally mild winters. Snowfall is light except in the high, mountainous regions where there is a heavier accumulation. The growing season is long and there is abundant rainfall, more than 45 inches annually.

Nathan Bedford Forrest
Probably the greatest Confederate cavalryman; commanded cavalry units in Tennessee

John Sevier
Frontiersman, governor of the independent State of Franklin, and the first governor of Tennessee

Tennessee, bounded by eight states, lies between the Appalachian Mountains on the east and the Mississippi River on the west. The state, which is four times as wide, east and west, as it is long, divides naturally into three geographic sections—East, Middle, and West Tennessee, and each is quite different from the other two.

In East Tennessee are the high mountains—the Unakas and the Great Smokies, which straddle the North Carolina line—the Great Valley, and the Cumberland Plateau. The Great Valley here is usually called the East Tennessee Valley because the Tennessee River flows through it.

Important Whens and Whats in the Making of Tennessee

1540   Spanish explorer Hernando de Soto reaches the Tennessee region.

1682   La Salle claims the Mississippi Valley for France.

1763   The region is part of the territory ceded to England after the French and Indian War.

1769   The first permanent white settlement is made in the Watauga Valley.

1775   The Wilderness Road is built through the Cumberland Gap.

1784-1788   Settlers form the "state" of Franklin.

1790   North Carolina cedes the Tennessee region to the federal government. The region becomes part of the "Territory South of the River Ohio."

1796   Tennessee is admitted to the Union as the 16th state.

1861   Tennessee secedes from the Union and joins the Confederacy.

1866   Tennessee is readmitted to the Union.

For generations the mountain folks lived in East Tennessee, isolated from the rest of the world. Until the TVA came, building dams and lakes and bringing roads and industry and people, the mountain folks worked their patches of ground in mountain cove and valley by primitive means and traveled the mountain trails on foot or muleback. Some of them still cling to their old ways and resent the coming of new people and new ways.

Major industrial plants—chemicals, textiles, metal products, and food processing—are in East Tennessee. This area is popular with tourists, too, because of its great scenic beauty. Principal cities are Knoxville, near the Great Smoky Mountains National Park, and Chattanooga, on the famous Moccasin Bend of the Tennessee River near Lookout and Signal mountains and Missionary Ridge.

The Tennessee River leaves the Great Valley and swings west through northern Alabama; it then loops north through western Tennessee on its way to Kentucky and the Ohio River. This loop, part of which is now the huge Kentucky Lake, forms the west boundary of Middle Tennessee, a fertile bluegrass area underlaid with limestone. This region is famous for its dark tobacco and fine livestock—horses, including the famous Tennessee Walking Horse, mules, and dairy cattle. Nashville, capital of the state, centers the area, and there are many handsome old southern mansions.

West Tennessee lies between the Tennessee and the Mississippi rivers. In this region of rugged hills, fertile valleys, and rich, black river bottoms, most of the state's cotton is grown. Memphis, the state's largest city and an important port on the Mississippi River, is an international cotton market, and the Cotton Carnival is held here every May.

Tennessee has given three Presidents to the nation—Andrew Jackson, James Knox Polk, and Andrew Johnson. After the Civil War started, the state seceded from the Union and joined the Confederacy, and several hundred battles were fought on Tennessee soil. In some of these, members of the same family fought against each other, for there were many Union sympathizers in the state. Tennessee was the first state to be readmitted to the Union, on March 23, 1866.

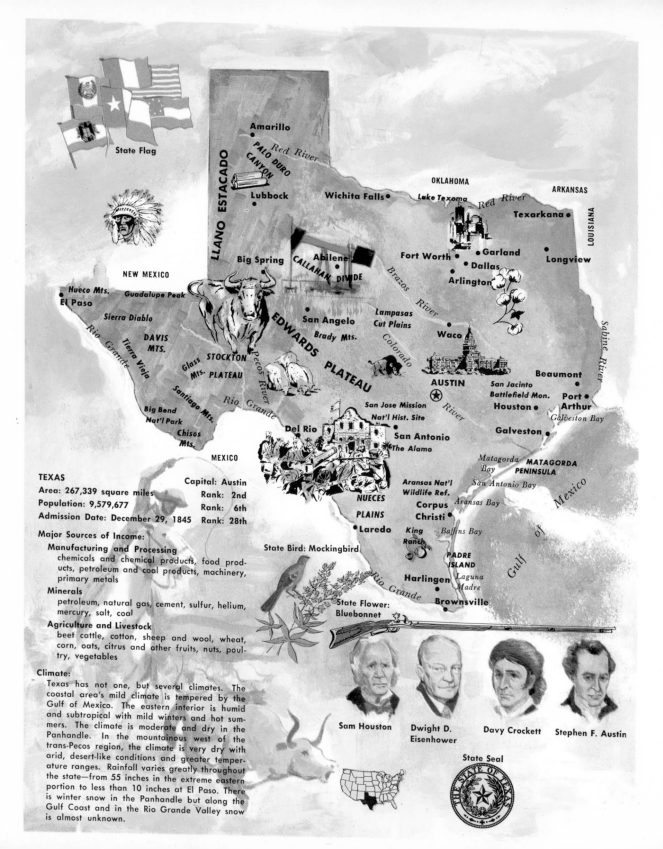

State Flag

Amarillo

Red River

PALO DURO CANYON

Lubbock

Wichita Falls

Lake Texoma

Red River

OKLAHOMA

ARKANSAS

LOUISIANA

Texarkana

LLANO ESTACADO

Big Spring

CALLAHAN DIVIDE

Abilene

Fort Worth

Garland

Dallas

Longview

Arlington

NEW MEXICO

Hueco Mts.

Guadalupe Peak

El Paso

Sierra Diablo

DAVIS MTS.

Tierra Vieja

Rio Grande

Glass Mts.

STOCKTON PLATEAU

Pecos River

Santiago Mts.

Big Bend Nat'l Park

Chisos Mts.

Rio Grande

San Angelo

Brady Mts.

Lampasas Cut Plains

EDWARDS PLATEAU

Colorado

Brazos River

Waco

AUSTIN

Sabine River

Beaumont

San Jacinto Battlefield Mon.

Houston

Port Arthur

Galveston Bay

MEXICO

Del Rio

San Jose Mission Nat'l Hist. Site

San Antonio

The Alamo

River

Galveston

Matagorda Bay

MATAGORDA PENINSULA

San Antonio Bay

Aransas Nat'l Wildlife Ref.

Aransas Bay

NUECES PLAINS

Corpus Christi

Gulf

of

Mexico

Laredo

King Ranch

Baffins Bay

State Bird: Mockingbird

PADRE ISLAND

Harlingen

Laguna Madre

Rio Grande

State Flower: Bluebonnet

Brownsville

TEXAS

Area: 267,339 square miles

Population: 9,579,677

Admission Date: December 29, 1845

Capital: Austin

Rank: 2nd

Rank: 6th

Rank: 28th

Major Sources of Income:
  Manufacturing and Processing
    chemicals and chemical products, food prod-
    ucts, petroleum and coal products, machinery,
    primary metals
  Minerals
    petroleum, natural gas, cement, sulfur, helium,
    mercury, salt, coal
  Agriculture and Livestock
    beef cattle, cotton, sheep and wool, wheat,
    corn, oats, citrus and other fruits, nuts, poul-
    try, vegetables

Climate:
    Texas has not one, but several climates. The
    coastal area's mild climate is tempered by the
    Gulf of Mexico. The eastern interior is humid
    and subtropical with mild winters and hot sum-
    mers. The climate is moderate and dry in the
    Panhandle. In the mountainous west of the
    trans-Pecos region, the climate is very dry with
    arid, desert-like conditions and greater temper-
    ature ranges. Rainfall varies greatly throughout
    the state—from 55 inches in the extreme eastern
    portion to less than 10 inches at El Paso. There
    is winter snow in the Panhandle but along the
    Gulf Coast and in the Rio Grande Valley snow
    is almost unknown.

Sam Houston

Dwight D. Eisenhower

Davy Crockett

Stephen F. Austin

State Seal

Texas, the largest state until Alaska entered the Union, is as big as Illinois, Ohio, Pennsylvania, New Jersey, New York, and the six New England states combined. It is unique because it is the only state to have entered the Union as an independent nation instead of as a territory, and it has numerous "firsts." It leads the nation in the production of petroleum, natural gas, and sulfur. It grows more cotton and beef cattle, produces more wool and mohair (the hair of Angora goats), and often produces more pecans than any other state.

Important Whens and Whats in the Making of Texas

1519	Alvarez de Pineda explores the coastal area.
1528	Cabeza de Vaca's ship is wrecked off the Texas coast.
1541	Coronado crosses the region in search of gold.
1681-1682	The Spanish build a mission and the first town is settled at Ysleta.
1685	The Frenchman La Salle builds Fort St. Louis.
1691	Texas becomes a Spanish province.
1821	When Mexico wins independence from Spain, Texas becomes a Mexican state; Stephen F. Austin brings in American settlers.
1836	After the revolt of the American settlers and the fall of the Alamo, the defeat of the Mexicans at San Jacinto wins Texas independence from Mexico, the Republic of Texas is formed.
1845	After voting for annexation to the United States, Texas is admitted to the Union as the 28th state.
1861	Texas secedes from the Union and joins the Confederacy.
1870	Texas is readmitted to the Union.

The trans-Pecos region, with its rugged mountains, canyons, and deserts, juts westward along the southern boundary of New Mexico, and the famous Rio Grande forms the entire boundary with Mexico. The state's panhandle pushes north between New Mexico and Oklahoma to Oklahoma's slender panhandle.

Except for the trans-Pecos region, the state is largely rolling plains that rise from the Gulf Coastal Plain and the interior lowlands to the Western High Plains. The rivers generally flow south or southeastward, eventually to drain into the Rio Grande, the Gulf of Mexico, or the Mississippi.

Eastern Texas, with its high humidity, is quite unlike the drier western half; it is more like its deep-South neighbor, Louisiana. The lower Rio Grande Valley is noted for its citrus fruits, palm trees, royal poincianas, and other subtropical plants.

The cities and towns along the Gulf Coast have become popular as summer and winter resorts because of their pleasant climate, miles of bathing beaches, and deep-sea fishing. The only known flock of whooping cranes winters at the Aransas National Wildlife Refuge, near Corpus Christi. Parks are being established on Padre Island and other barrier islands along the coast, whose quiet lagoons form part of the Intra-coastal Waterway.

During her more than four centuries of history, the flags of six nations have flown over Texas—those of France, Spain, Mexico, the Republic of Texas, the United States, and the Confederacy—and there are historic shrines and relics throughout the state. The town of Ysleta, near El Paso, in the extreme western corner of the state, was founded by the Spanish in 1682. San Jacinto State Park, on the Houston Ship Canal, contains the San Jacinto Battlefield, with its 570-foot monument, and the battleship *U.S.S. Texas.* Huntsville has the home, law office, and burial place of General Sam Houston. The Alamo, originally the Mission San Antonio de Valero, is at San Antonio, and so are the Spanish Governors' Palace and the Mission San José, now a national historic site.

From San Antonio north to the Colorado River is a highly scenic resort area known as the Hill and Highland Lakes Country. The lakes, one of which is in the city of Austin, are formed by dams on the Colorado River. Another popular resort area is huge Lake Texoma on the Oklahoma border, backed up behind a dam across the Red River near Denison. Former President Dwight Eisenhower's birthplace at Denison has been restored and is now a historic shrine.

Glossary

arid (ăr′ĭd) without moisture; dry; barren.

aristocracy (ăr′ĭs tŏk′rȧ sĭ) 1. the nobles or chief persons in a state; a privileged class; 2. those regarded as superior to the rest of the community, as in rank, wealth, or intellect.

artifact (är′tĭ făkt) a product of human workmanship, especially of primitive skill.

bauxite (bôks′īt) an iron substance, consisting of several minerals occurring in some limestone masses and in earthy forms.

bromide (brō′mīd) a compound made of the bromine vapor and other elements much used in medicine and in photography.

broomcorn (broom′kôrn′) a tall sorghum which has a jointed stem with long stiff-branched spires, used for making brooms and brushes.

carat (kăr′ăt) a unit of weight for precious stones.

cede (sēd) to yield, grant, or give; also to assign.

culture (kŭl′tūr) 1. a particular stage in the development of a civilization; 2. the characteristic features of such a stage.

descendant (dė sĕn′dănt) one who descends, as an offspring; the opposite of ancestor.

drought (drout) 1. dryness; in need of rain; 2. a dry spell.

extinct (ĕks tĭngkt′) no longer living or active; that which has died out; as an animal or plant.

fossil (fŏs′ĭl) any impression or trace, of an animal or plant of the past, which has been preserved in the earth's crust.

giant sloth (jī′ănt slōth) a very large, slow-moving mammal which stays on the ground—found in tropical forests.

gristmill (grĭst′mĭl) a mill for grinding grain.

hacienda (ä syän′dä; hăs′ĭ ĕn′dȧ) a large estate.

irrigate (ĭr′ĭ gāt) to supply land with water by causing a stream to flow on, over, or through it, as in artificial channels.

lore (lōr) knowledge, learning; often that knowledge which is possessed by an entire group or class.

mammoth (măm′ŭth) 1. an elephant no longer living, known by its large teeth and cement-like material between the teeth; 2. referring to size—being very large.

mastodon (măs′tȯ dŏn) an elephant-like animal which is no longer living, differing from a mammoth in the molar teeth.

migration (mī grā′shŭn) 1. the act of moving from one place to another, with the intention of establishing residence. 2. to pass periodically from one region or climate to another for feeding or breeding, as some birds and animals.

navigable (năv′ĭ gȧ b'l) capable of being used by ships and vessels—deep enough and wide enough to allow boats to pass through.

nomad (nō′măd) a race or tribe that has no fixed location, but wanders.

prey (prā) 1. any animal seized by another to be eaten; 2. the act of seizing; 3. to make raids for the sake of steal-

90

ing, to seek or take food or victims.

replica (rĕp'lĭ kȧ) a reproduction or copy, as of a picture or statue.

resin (rĕz'ĭn) an unshaped solid or partly solid natural organic substance mainly of plant origin. It is usually yellowish to dark brown, sometimes transparent and not soluble in water.

secede (sė sēd') to withdraw from an organization, communion or federation; especially, to withdraw formally from a political or religious body.

sediment (sĕd'ĭ mĕnt) the matter which settles to the bottom from a liquid; material left after water has receded.

sluice gate (slo͞os gāt) the gate of an artificial stream of water used in regulating water for irrigation purposes; a water gate or floodgate.

sovereign (sŏv'ēr ĭn; sŏv'rĭn) 1. chief or highest, supreme; 2. supreme in power, superior in position to all others; 3. independent of any other authority or jurisdiction.

stalactite (stȧ lăk'tīt) a deposit of calcium carbonate, resembling an icicle, hanging from the roof or sides of a cavern. It is formed by the continuous dripping of water mixed with calcium carbonate. As the moisture evaporates a deposit is left to form the downward peak.

stalagmite (stȧ lăg'mīt) a deposit of calcium carbonate formed on the floor of a cavern as a result of the continuous formation of a stalactite.

sulfur (sŭl'fēr) a yellowish non-metallic element occurring in crystals, masses, crusts, or powder which burns in air with a blue flame and intense odor. It is used in making gunpowder and matches, vulcanizing rubber, and in medicines and ointments.

Tennessee Valley Authority—a government agency, created by Act of Congress to develop the Tennessee River system for the purposes of flood control, navigation, and the creation of water power; to generate and sell surplus electricity, to develop fertilizers and to aid in soil conservation.

topography (tȯ pŏg'rȧ fĭ) the figure or pattern of a surface, including its relief, the position of its streams, lakes, roads, cities, etc.

Grateful acknowledgment is made to the following for the helpful information and materials furnished by them used in the preparation of this book:

United States Department of the Interior, National Park Service; particularly the national parks of Big Bend, Great Smoky Mountains, Hot Springs, Mammoth Cave and Platt, and their respective managements.

United States Department of Commerce, Bureau of the Census, Field Services, Chicago, Illinois.

State of Alabama Bureau of Publicity and Information.

State of Alabama Planning and Industrial Development Board.

Arkansas Publicity and Parks Commission.

Hot Springs Chamber of Commerce.

Kentucky Tourist and Travel Commission.

State of Louisiana Department of Commerce and Industry.

Mississippi Agricultural and Industrial Board.

Oklahoma Planning and Resources Board.

Tennessee Division of Information and Tourist Promotion, Department of Conservation and Commerce.

Texas Highway Department, Travel and Information Division

International Visual Educational Services, Inc., Chicago, Illinois.

Index

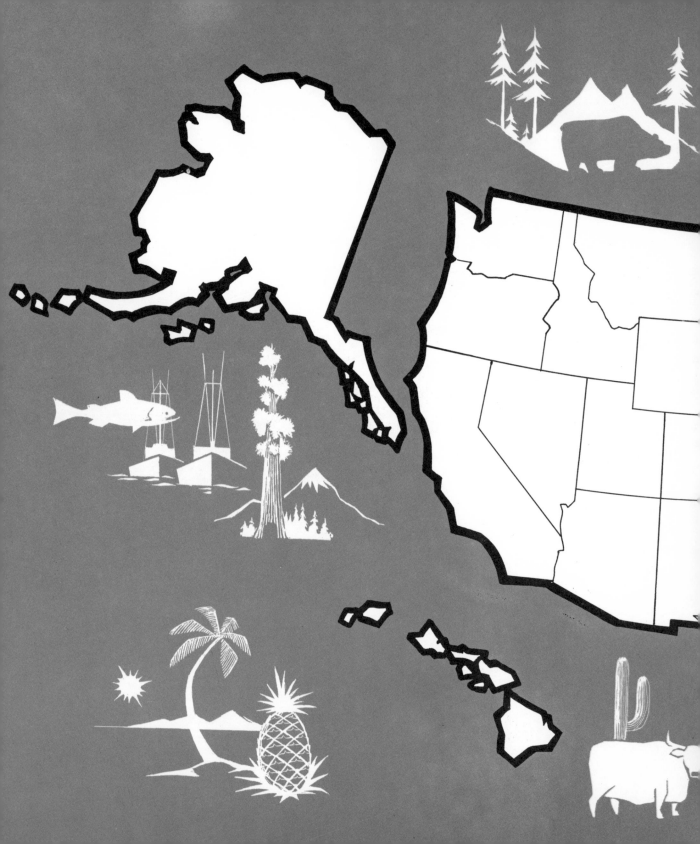